D0399323

INVESTING IN
GOLD

INVESTING IN
GOLD

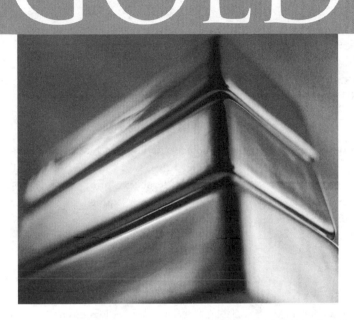

THE ESSENTIAL SAFE HAVEN
INVESTMENT FOR EVERY PORTFOLIO

JONATHAN SPALL

New York   Chicago   San Francisco   Lisbon   London
Madrid   Mexico City   Milan   New Delhi   San Juan
Seoul   Singapore   Sydney   Toronto

The **McGraw·Hill** Companies

Copyright © 2009 by Jonathan Spall. All rights reserved. Printed in the United States of America. Except as permitted under the United States Copyright Act of 1976, no part of this publication may be reproduced or distributed in any form or by any means, or stored in a data base or retrieval system, without prior written permission of the publisher.

1 2 3 4 5 6 7 8 9 0   DOC/DOC   0 1 0 9 8

ISBN: 978–0–07–160346–1
MHID: 0–07–160346–8

This publication is designed to provide accurate and authoritative information in regard to the subject matter covered. It is sold with the understanding that the publisher is not engaged in rendering legal, accounting, or other professional service. If legal advice or other expert assistance is required, the services of a competent professional person should be sought.

—From a Declaration of Principles Jointly Adopted
by a Committee of the American Bar Association
and a Committee of Publishers and Associations

McGraw-Hill books are available at special quantity discounts to use as premiums and sales promotions, or for use in corporate training programs. To contact a representative, please visit the Contact Us pages at www.mhprofessional.com.

This book is printed on acid-free paper.

This book is dedicated
with much love to
my parents, Kay and Jack,
my wife Cynthia,
and our children,
Alex and Charlotte.

Contents

Acknowledgments

Given that this book is a chronological journey through the life of gold, it makes sense to treat the acknowledgments in the same way. Therefore, I first need to thank my parents: my father for instilling a love of the gold market in me—indeed, I segued flawlessly from a desperate desire to be a train driver or an astronaut into wanting to "be like him" (a gold trader) by the time my age hit double figures— and my mother for allowing long Sunday lunches where the relative merits of long or short positions were debated; doubtless to the despair of her and my sister.

Moving rapidly up to date, I have to apologize to my wife and children for spending far too much time at the office generally and more recently tapping away one-fingered on a laptop in the kitchen trying to complete this book; in the process neglecting helping with homework, walking the dog, and all those other duties that make up normal family life.

In my 25 years of working in the gold market I have encountered people whom I deeply respected and enjoyed the opportunity to learn from as well as those who should not have been allowed out to buy a newspaper, let alone being entrusted with multimillion-dollar positions. While it is difficult to single out individuals for praise—let alone dangerous to pick those for derision—I would like to thank Ed Hofstatter (Sharps Pixley), David Saunders and

Colin Griffith (Credit Suisse), Peter Hillyard (Chase Manhattan), Fritz Plass, Mike Nutt, and John Pacilio (Deutsche Bank), and Benoit de Vitry (Barclays Capital), all of whom have been my bosses at various stages of my career.

To my many colleagues, friends, and competitors in the market, I would like to offer my wholehearted thanks for the banter and the sparring as we tried to beat each other up during the trading day and yet managed friendship and socializing after work. You are too numerous to mention individually so I am not even going to bother to try. However, these people are based all over the world and extend from my 16 years of working in the London market, through to 6 years in Hong Kong, and 3 years in Sydney. You made it all worthwhile!

It would be nice to think that in my time in this industry I had developed total recall and a perfect knowledge, sadly untrue. As such I have had to search back through my notes and recollections before ultimately approaching a number of people in the business for assistance with data and information.

In this respect I would particularly like to thank Suki Cooper from the Commodity Research team at Barclays Capital as well as Jill Leyland of the World Gold Council for their patience and help in dealing with my many queries.

I also am grateful for the assistance of Mark Lynam and Alan Fine of AngloGold Ashanti; George Milling-Stanley and Matthew Graydon of the World Gold Council; Paul Walker of GFMS; Jessica Cross and her team at Virtual Metals; Andy Smith of Ridgefield Capital; Paul Fisher from the Bank of England; Johan Botha of the Rand Refinery; and Stewart Murray and Suzanne Capano, both of the LBMA.

I also thank the International Monetary Fund (Patricia Loo), the European Central Bank (Regina Schuller), Dennis Gartman, TOCOM (Tony Crane), NYMEX (Jenifer Semenza), The Chinese Gold and Silver Exchange Society (Cynthia Chan), Shanghai Futures Exchange (Cui Tong), Dubai Commodity Exchange (Colin Griffith), Barclays Global Investors (Joshua Roberts), and The London Gold Market Fixing Ltd.

Acknowledgments

In addition, I would like to thank GATA (Chris Powell), No Dirty Gold (Payal Sampat), and ARM (Catalina Cock).

Of my colleagues at Barclays Capital, I would like to thank Kevin Rush, Troy Bowler, Ted Morris, Yu Yingxi, Marc Booker, Martyn Whitehead, Konstantinos Katsigiannakis, Ralph Segreti, Will Bowen, and Peh Chin Yang.

Finally, I would like to thank Jeanne Glasser and her colleagues at McGraw-Hill for their support and encouragement during this undertaking.

Thank you all for your assistance and encouragement. Of course the errors are mine entirely!

INVESTING IN
GOLD

Introduction

In this book, you'll find no analysis of why Egyptian pharaohs had gold death masks or if pre-Colombian civilizations might have used prodigious quantities of gold. Nor is there debate as to the magical or medicinal quantities of this most sought after of metals. What you will discover, however, is how the gold market functions, terminology used by traders and what influences the decisions they make. This book is written for the broadest possible spectrum of those interested in precious metals, from private individuals to central banks, from mining companies to hedge funds. The writing style is intended to make this book approachable to many different types of readers.

This book is based on first-hand knowledge of the market and avoids academic discussion. I draw upon the experience I have gained working in a trading room for a living. I started my full-time career in the gold market in 1983. Apart from the odd foray as a foreign exchange and bond trader, this is what I have spent my working life doing—trading and talking to customers about precious metals markets. Over the last 25 years or so, I have worked for four of the world's largest banks and always for those that have had a strong position in this market. To stretch the history even farther, I have spent a number of school vacations working in the industry as well, and I was lucky enough to spend time on Wall Street in 1980, when gold was trading at its then all-time highs.

During my career I have lived and worked in New York, London, Hong Kong, and Sydney. I have been an interbank market maker on three continents and have traveled to 70 or so nations to meet with central banks and finance ministries to discuss the outlook for gold. I have sat with mining companies to debate hedging strategies and traveled over a mile underground to see the ore being extracted. Currently the majority of my time is spent talking to those involved with hedge, pension, and sovereign wealth funds on the events surrounding the recent extraordinary rise in the metal's price.

I have previously written books on the working of the market for my employers that have only been handed out to major clients. However, this is the first time that one of my publications has been made generally available. It contains information backed up by personal experience; it may not conform to an academic view of how markets should operate, but it does closely mirror the terminology and thought processes of those who work in this field for a living.

The book is basically laid out to describe gold's journey from being mined and refined, to the trading process (the bulk of the book), and ultimately to the world's physical markets (jewelry, investment bars, and so on). Although readers can work their way through the entire publication, each of the chapters is intended as a self-contained episode and can be read in isolation.

The Book in Brief

Throughout the book I have assumed a basic level of knowledge of the jargon used in markets. However, there is also a glossary of terms in Appendix III that should help to clear up any confusion if it arises.

The first section of the book looks at the gold mining industry. It describes how metal is extracted (open pit and underground mining being the major methods), the challenges facing the producers, be it from the logistics involved in working deep beneath the Earth's surface or from environmentalists, as well as the ways in which mining companies have tried to mitigate their financial risks. Hedging is obviously no longer an option for many mining companies, but their traditional stance in the market is clearly important when debating the price history and outlook for gold.

When writing about refining metal, I am going to take a broad approach. This involves not just the activities of refiners but also the activities undertaken by mining companies in the first stages of gold's journey from being a chunk of rather unattractive rock to an adornment worn by some of the world's most celebrated people. I will also discuss how the metal is moved around the world to achieve this. However, the most important part is the London Good Delivery bars—the benchmark by which all bullion is judged.

After that, it is the turn of central banks, or the "official sector" as it is sometimes described, a soubriquet that brings in governments and sovereign wealth funds as well. This chapter looks at why central banks hold gold, the activities that they undertake in the market, and finally, are they likely to buy more metal. It is this last area that is the biggest cause for debate, which very often brings some of the most misguided and least intelligent "analysis" of the market. Having met with senior staff at all the world's largest holders of gold, I am keen to clarify the concerns and responsibilities of this key sector.

Banks that operate in the gold market are often referred to as simply "bullion banks." It is not a title that I particularly care for; however, it is a title that is widely used. On this occasion I have taken the path of least resistance and employed this as the title for the chapter on interbank trading, essentially an explanation of how the market operates and with an analysis of liquidity, terminology, gold interest rates, and the London gold fixing.

While the various exchanges on which gold is traded form an integral part of the everyday activity of the bullion banks, I opted to write about them in a separate chapter because of the wide interest in these institutions, particularly since for some market participants this is the only market that they know, choosing never to get involved in over-the-counter (OTC) trading.

Similarly, exchange-traded funds (ETFs) could have been included in Chapter 7, which discusses gold exchanges. Here again, though, this relatively new innovation for precious metals markets has had an enormous impact on gold investment and deserves a chapter of its own.

The final piece of gold's journey is in the physical market, whether it is as jewelry or in small bar form. Indeed in a number of countries there is no real difference between the two; certainly in Asia buying gold is often devoid of the sentimentality that characterizes its purchase in the majority of Western nations. This lack of emotion helps in understanding the notion of scrap gold.

Having traced gold's journey from "rock to ring," I then concentrate on the myths and reality of the gold market as well as the metal's relevance to today's world, while focusing on the reasons behind gold's rise to all-time nominal highs.

The final chapter is a summary of the various ways in which investors can seek to gain exposure to gold and provides a summary of the advantages, or otherwise, of each.

To assist in an overall understanding I have put together a few FAQs, a glossary of the market, as well as a conversion table, and a short piece on the properties of gold.

Gold Mining

⊰ Who Mines Gold? ⊱

 South Africa is synonymous with gold, and it is generally assumed that it is the world's largest producer. Except that it no longer is. The nation that is responsible for roughly one-third of all gold ever mined, and which was producing 1,000 or so metric tonnes per annum of the metal in 1970, is now only mining around 270 tonnes a year.*

In the second half of 2007, South Africa was overtaken by China for the first time, and China is now the world's biggest producer. Indeed South African production has declined at some 5.6 percent per annum for the last decade. Similarly, Australia, which had been on an upward trajectory for much of the 1990s, has found its output slipping recently.

However, gold remains vital to the South African economy, still providing employment to some 160,000 people, according

---

*Throughout this book I have used the spelling tonnes rather than tons to refer to metric tons, because tonne is the term used globally in the gold market, and because the spelling ton is ambiguous; it could refer either to the metric ton, the American short ton, or the British long ton, which are three rather different quantities. The term tonne, however, is unambiguous in that it always refers to the metric ton.

to South Africa's Chamber of Mines. As to how many people further depend on gold mining—that is a rather more difficult question. It is thought that there are some 5 million dependents of 458,600 employees in all types of mining—a ratio of nearly 11 to 1. Generally the figure is muddled by multiple marriages, which means that the overall number is anywhere between 5 and 12 dependents for each miner. Realistically then, there are around 1,500,000 people who survive because of wages from the South African gold mining industry.

Unsurprisingly, similar to production figures, employment has been falling at roughly 8 percent per annum on average for the last five years. To put this into perspective, the peak was reached in 1987 when *Gold in South Africa* reported that 530,622 were employed. Gold is the country's second largest export earner after platinum group metals (or "PGMs" as they are more generally referred to).

So exactly what was produced by which country in 2007? See Table 1–1.

Table 1–1
Gold Production by Country in 2007

COUNTRY	2007 PRODUCTION (IN TONNES)
China	280.5
South Africa	269.9
Australia	246.3
United States	239.5
Peru	169.6
Russia	169.2
Indonesia	146.7
Canada	101.2
Uzbekistan	75.3
Ghana	75.1

© GFMS Gold Survey, 2008.

Gold Mining

GFMS estimates that the total global mine production was 2,475.9 tonnes for 2007.

The leading companies that have been extracting the metal on a worldwide basis are listed in Table 1–2.

Table 1–2
Leading Worldwide Gold Extractors

MINING COMPANIES	2007 PRODUCTION (TONNES)
Barrick Gold	250.7
AngloGold Ashanti	170.4
Newmont Mining	165.6
Gold Fields	122.9
Freeport McMoRan	71.6

Source: From various company reports and GFMS. Copyright © GFMS Gold Survey, 2008.

The romantic notion of gold mining is that the metal is found in glittering lumps. However, the truth is considerably less exciting, with companies forced to move enormous quantities of material to extract the mineral.

The two main types of mining are open pit and underground, with the former being more prevalent in North America and Australia and the latter predominant in South Africa. However, some mines start off as open pit when the ore is relatively easy to access before switching to underground as the mine matures.

Gold deposits have been worked for many thousands of years—with some evidence to suggest that the Egyptians were mining underground as long ago as 2000 B.C., with rivers being "plundered" for gold nuggets even earlier. In essence little has changed over the last few thousand years with underground and open pit being the major forms of mining, it is simply the scale and technology used, which are beyond all recognition.

⊸ Underground Mining ⊱

Some years ago, I was fortunate enough to be allowed to visit the Tau Tona mine (the name means "great lion" in Sesotho), operated by AngloGold Ashanti, which is located about 40 miles outside Johannesburg. This was very much a visit to a working mine rather than a VIP trip to a showpiece. After long safety briefings—including no use of mobile phones, cameras, etc., without permission to ensure that we did not accidentally set off explosives—we were taken one and one-quarter miles underground. The mine itself goes even deeper with ore being extracted at an average depth of almost two miles and at its deepest point descends a further one-third of a mile. At over two miles deep this is still not the deepest mine in the world. This honor currently belongs to Gold Fields' Driefontein Mine at over two and one-half miles deep (4,121 meters), followed by their Kloof Mine at just about two and one-half miles (4,020 meters). These records may not last long as gold deposits have been identified as deep as three and one-half miles underground, and although the technology is sufficiently advanced to exploit these deposits, the extraction costs remain prohibitive—at least currently.

To get the personnel to their jobs underground, a series of rapid elevators is used. These elevators are typically triple-deckers that can take a total of 120 people and travel at the equivalent of 37 miles per hour or 3,000 feet per minute.

I was not sure what to expect while one and one-quarter miles underground, but I fell for the common mistake of believing that the glittering gold-colored flecks were the ore lode rather than being classic fool's gold (pyrite), whereas the dull gray rocks are what I should have been impressed by: the reason for drilling down so deep below the Earth's surface.

This "Carbon Leader Reef" contains gold in carbon. What this designation actually means is that in the gray rock are a series of white "pebbles." These "pebbles" look like specks of marble, but are actually quartz that is dotted around. Surrounding each of these pieces of quartz is a tiny circle of black, among the general dark gray, no more than one millimeter thick. It is in these tiny bands, over a mile underground, where the "gold in carbon" is found.

The reef itself can vary from just an inch wide to more than 10 feet wide. However, it is not practical to mine seams less than three feet thick.

Geology

More formally, AngloGold Ashanti describes the reef as follows:

> The Witwatersrand Basin comprises a 6 kilometer thick sequence of interbedded argillaceous and are nacreous sediments that extend laterally for some 300 kilometers northeast/southwest and 100 kilometers northwest/southeast on the Kaapval Cratan. The upper portion of the basin, which contains the ore bodies, outcrops at its northern extent near Johannesburg. Further west, south, and east, the basin is overlain by up to four kilometers of Archean, Proterozoic, and Mesozoic volcanic and sedimentary rocks. The Witwatersrand Basin is late Archean in age and is considered to be around 2.7 billion to 2.8 billion years old. Gold occurs in laterally extensive quartz pebble conglomerate horizons or reefs, which are generally less than 2 meters thick and are widely considered to represent laterally extensive braided fluvial deposits. The Carbon Leader Reef (CLR) consists of one or more conglomerate units and varies from several centimeters to more than three meters in thickness.

Working Practices

Work continues around the clock at these enormous enterprises. Each day shift involves drilling and supporting the advancing stope face, the South African term for the working area of the mine. Each stope face is advanced at an average of three feet per day. It is cleaned, prepared for drilling, charged with explosives (in the form of ammonium nitrate fuel oil), and then connected through a series of detonators and blasting wires. Charges are set off approximately one hour after miners leave the face.

The night shift commences four hours after blasting fumes have been removed via the ventilation system, and a crew of winch drivers and locomotive operators scrape the stope face and advancing gullies into holes in preparation for the day shift to repeat the process.

These holes, known as box holes, are equipped with a chute. From here the ore is transferred to open rail carts called "hoppers," which are then hauled by locomotives to the shaft area. The rock is dropped through a series of large openings or "ore passes" from which it falls to the deepest levels of the mine. It is then loaded into the shaft skips and hoisted to the surface.

Clearly, transporting huge amounts of raw material to a refinery would be an enormous logistical effort. Hence the initial upgrading is done on-site. So once the ore reaches the surface, it is moved to the processing plant by rail or conveyor belt, whereupon it is crushed and treated by chemicals to extract the gold. The purity level at this point is still low (around 60 percent). To further refine it, the gold solution is poured into cathode moulds and smelted in a furnace to produce bars of roughly 90 percent purity. These doré bars are then shipped to a specialist refinery to create the finished product—a topic discussed in more depth in Chapter 2.

Reserves and Resources

While this description gives some idea of the working practices, it does not give an idea of the sheer scale of the enterprise. A mine like Tau Tona could have upward of 5,000 employees and have reserves of some 19 million tonnes. Of course, this amount is not millions of tonnes of gold, but rather of ore, which would yield some 6.5 million ounces of gold (just 200 tonnes), assuming a rich seam of 10 to 11 grams of gold per tonne of ore. It takes roughly three tonnes of ore to mine one ounce of gold on this basis.

In contrast to reserves, which are likely to be extracted, a mine of this size would have further resources, which have the potential of being exploited should the gold price to technology offset be favorable. These resources might run to a further 20 million tonnes or so.

While these are enormous, almost inconceivable amounts of ore—and all this merely from one mine—there are other challenges to mining at deep levels.

Challenges of Underground Mining

Underground mining is difficult or dangerous due to these factors:

- *Seismicity:* Being so deep underground, the frequent occurrence of earthquakes, which often manifest as rock bursts, poses an ever-present danger to mine workers and equipment.

- *Temperature:* As you go deeper, it gets hotter. At Tau Tona, AngloGold Ashanti is using huge refrigeration units powered by 65 megawatts of power to bring the temperature down to levels at which people can work. Without this cooling, the ambient temperature would be higher than 122 degrees Fahrenheit.

- *Gas:* In particular, miners are threatened by the buildup of noxious gases—carbon dioxide (CO_2) and methane (CH_4)—which are derived from coal. This accumulation often occurs at shallow depths in South African gold mines and results in their classification as "fiery mines."

◦⟩ Open Pit ⟨◦

While I could have picked a completely different company to look at to discuss open pit mining, I decided to stay with AngloGold Ashanti for the sake of continuity. In fact, AngloGold Ashanti has only one operation in the United States, the Cripple Creek and Victor (CCV) mine in Colorado. In contrast to some 5,000 employees or so at Tau Tona, this open pit mine has a workforce of fewer than 400 employees, but it produced 283,000 ounces of gold in 2006—some 767 ounces of gold per person employed compared to fewer than 100 ounces per person at a typical underground mine like Tau Tona.

Indeed, this was a 14 percent production decrease compared to the previous year, due to drought. Looking at 2005 figures, the difference is even more stark, equating to roughly 860 ounces of gold per employee. However, extracting the 329,625 ounces of gold that were produced required that over 20 million tonnes of ore be processed, involving an additional 40 million tonnes of overburden and other material. In other words, each ounce of gold required over 60 tonnes of ore to be milled and treated, clearly much lower yields than those from underground mining, aptly demonstrating the very much more labor- and capital-intensive nature of deep level gold production.

Geology

The Cripple Creek and Victor gold mine's Web site (www.ccvgold mining.com) goes into much detail about the history of mineralization in the area. The salient points, as outlined there are:

> The gold presently being mined is generally less than 20 microns in size and occurs in three principal forms: native gold associated with pyrite as embayments or replacements along the margins of the pyrite grains and in some cases intergrown with pyrite; as native gold associated with hydrous iron and manganese oxides after tellurides; as gold-silver tellurides primarily in quartz-fluorite veins. Oxidation is strongest and deepest along major structural zones. In general, oxidation of the deposit has a nominal depth of 122 meters (400 feet).

Working Practices

Cripple Creek and Victor was originally mined for its rich underground seam. Once this ran out, the attention switched to the above-ground, low-yield ore, where mining takes place 24 hours every day of the year.

Drill holes are bored then loaded for blasting with ammonium nitrate and a fuel mixture. This favored mixture is not explosive until detonated with a booster. The rock is taken from the mine site in 300-tonne capacity trucks. Again according to the CCV Web site, the material is separated into "overburden" (the material overlying an ore deposit), which is hauled to storage areas where no mining is slated to take place, whereas "the ore is transported to a two-stage crusher that produces coarse gravel measuring less than three-quarters of an inch at a rate of 3,000 tonnes per hour. Approximately 60,000,000 tonnes of material is moved annually."

At this point, lime is added to the gravel, which has the effect of raising the pH level and improving the effectiveness of heap leaching. This is a common process whereby "the naturally occurring metals, including gold and silver, that are exposed on the broken faces of the crushed ore are dissolved by a dilute sodium cyanide process solution." Clearly such a process requires enormous care because "the leaching of the gold is accomplished out-of-doors in a valley leach facility (VLF)—a valley area with clay and plastic liners upon which the crushed ore is placed for gold removal." The VLF can be thought of as a bathtub without a drain outlet, the sides and bottom of which are an impermeable double and triple liner system.

The crushed ore is placed in approximately 35-foot layers and a dilute solution of sodium cyanide, at 100 parts per million, is applied using buried agricultural-type drip-irrigation tubes to minimize evaporation. As this soaks through the ore, the process solution dissolves the gold and silver on the surface of the ore. The solution is captured at the lowest point of the VLF, the bathtub drain, and pumped into the recovery facility. The mixture containing gold is described as a "pregnant" solution. "Permits have been obtained that allow placement of about 300 million tonnes of ore on the valley leach facility."

From here the material "is pumped into the adsorption, desorption, and recovery (ADR) facility for recovery of the gold and silver."

"The solution is pumped through tanks containing activated carbon (roasted coconut shell) granules, which attract, or adsorb, the dissolved gold-cyanide complex. The process solution, now with no gold or "barren," is recirculated to the VLF to start the leaching cycle over. Process solution is pumped into and out of the ADR at a rate of 13,500 gallons per minute.

"Gold on the carbon is removed, or stripped, using a hot alkaline solution. The gold-rich solution is then piped to an electro-winning cell where direct electrical current is applied to attract metals from the solution to a stainless steel wool cathode, forming a solid, called mud, of gold, silver and impurities. The mud is sent to the refinery furnace and heated to separate the gold and silver from any non-metal substances." As in underground mining, the resulting doré bars are sent to a specialist refinery to convert to the finished product.

Challenges in Open Pit Mining

The challenges in open pit mining are significantly different from those for underground mining, where the risk of injury is far higher. Instead the issues with open pit mining are more about the sheer logistics of running a smooth operation 24 hours a day every day.

However, one risk associated with both of these types of mining, which I did not mention earlier, is the risk to the environment.

⋅∘⟨ The Environment ⟩∘⋅

Mining is not going to feature toward the top of the wish list for many environmentalists. Unsurprisingly the last few years have seen the rise of organizations such as No Dirty Gold and ARM (the Association for Responsible Mining).

The homepage of No Dirty Gold reads, "Gold mining is one of the dirtiest businesses in the world. The production of one gold ring generates 20 tonnes of mine waste." The campaign was launched in February 2004 by EARTHWORKS (formerly known as the Mineral Policy Centre) and Oxfam America, with the aim to "shake up the gold industry and change the way gold is mined." Since that time they have moved on to trying to develop "a system for independent verification of compliance with environmental and social standards for mining operations" as well as lobbying retailers to source "gold and precious metals from operations that meet these social and environmental criteria."

ARM has somewhat different aims and calls itself were "an independent, global-scale effort, and pioneer initiative, created as an international and multi-institutional organization to bring credibility, transparency and legitimacy to the development of a framework for responsible artisanal and small-scale mining." The organization is looking further to consumers to change their habits by means of educating "consumers as to their power to directly improve the quality of life of artisanal miners by purchasing fair trade jewellery and minerals."

The amount of "dirt" needing to be moved, the effect on the landscape, the chemical process, and the likely highlighted result as an adornment all can add fuel to the conservationists' fire. Furthermore, one of the chemicals involved is cyanide, increasing the combustibility of the argument very quickly. However, do these points address the issue fairly?

My first response to the question is that although the desire for solely small-scale "artisanal" mining is laudable, it runs parallel to the questions surrounding small-scale food production. Small-scale mining simply does not create enough supply to satiate demand. While the question of gold mining is nowhere near the magnitude of a problem as would be an essential input for human life such as food, we have largely managed to avoid the dire predictions of Thomas Malthus; there is still undoubtedly demand that cannot be stifled. In which case, this demand would likely be met with illegal mining and hence far more dire consequences for the environment with irresponsible use of exactly the same hazardous materials.

Second, while it is hard to argue that gold mining is an unalloyed blessing, simply highlighting that a lot of ore and overburden need to be processed for each ounce of gold is headline grabbing, but the enormous volumes do not convey the whole picture. As mentioned above, the industry employs some 160,000 individuals in South Africa alone; and each of these workers is depended on by an extended family. Multiply this throughout the world and the issue starts to look rather different. Admittedly in most of North America and Australia other employment opportunities exist, but this is not necessarily true within some of the emerging economies that produce gold, and equally it may not be true in rural Colorado.

Third, the mining companies have clearly realized that their industry needs to ensure that the highest standards are adhered to. This can vary from "environmental bonds" levied in countries such as Australia—requiring that before a mine is developed the gold producer has to lodge sufficient funds to return the mine site to its original, or improved, condition—to the long explanations of environmental impact mitigation that the industry is taking and that is listed in companies' annual reports. A few examples are:

1. At the Cripple Creek and Victor mine, "plans are underway to evaluate the possibility of harnessing the energy of the strong winds which always seem to be blowing …"

2. AngloGold Ashanti has made changes "to condenser tubes at all refrigeration units," for cooling underground mines, to prevent the release of R134a (a greenhouse gas).

3. Key indicators of environmental performance for AngloGold Ashanti are "the efficient use and management of cyanide, water, and energy. As well as the rehabilitation of 'disturbed lands' and the prevention of pollution."

It seems that we have moved a long way from Mark Twain's famous definition of a gold mine as "a hole in the ground owned by a liar."

Chapter 2 looks at the next stage in the chain, refining. However, in Chapter 3 I return to the mining companies to investigate their hedging activities.

Refining

 Once the gold has been mined, it is converted into doré bars, mostly at mine sites. These are of variable weight and quality with purities ranging from less than 50 percent to over 90 percent of gold. At this point they are of little use either to the jewelry trade or to institutions where gold represents quasi money; thus the need for specialist refineries. There are a large number of refineries around the world but only 58 that meet the London Bullion Market Association's good delivery list of acceptable refiners, which is the global benchmark.

The Rand Refinery, located just outside Johannesburg in the town of Germiston, is the world's largest single-site refining and smelting complex. Naturally it processes the vast majority of South Africa's production but it also refines approximately 80 percent of the continent's total production.

The initial treatment is via the Miller Chlorination Process: "This is a pyrometallurgical process whereby gold doré is heated in furnace crucibles. The process separates gold from impurities using chlorine gas, which is added to the crucibles once the gold has become molten. Chlorine gas does not react with gold but will combine with silver and base metals to form various chlorides. Once the chlorides have formed, they float to the surface as slag or escape as volatile gases. The surface melt and the fumes containing the impurities are collected and further refined to extract the gold and silver.

"This process can take up to 90 minutes and produces gold which is at least 99.5% pure with silver being the main remaining component."

Metal of this purity is then generally cast into London Good Delivery bars; more on that later in this chapter.

However, certain markets want metal of higher purity i.e., 99.99 percent, which is generally written as "9999" and referred to as "four nines gold," and bars smaller in size than the 400-ounce London Good Delivery bars. To achieve gold of that purity, the refined metal is cast into anodes and then sent to an electrolytic plant, where it is converted into gold sponge. However, in contrast to its name, this sponge is actually the metal in granular form, which is then resmelted into small "value-added" bars.

Because of local customs and traditions, the purity and size of bars vary among countries. Rand Refinery's gold production, for example, splits the world as shown in Table 2–1.

Table 2–1
Rand Refinery's Worldwide Gold Production

COUNTRY	PURITY	SIZE
India	99.50% or 99.90%	1,000 grams or 100 grams respectively
Turkey	99.50%	1,000 grams
Italy	99.99%	1,000 grams
Middle East	99.50%	1,000 grams
Far East (China, Taiwan)	99.99%	5 and 10 taels
Pakistan and Sri Lanka	99.90%	5 and 10 tolas

Source: ©Rand Refinery Ltd.

As shown, a wide range of measurements is used, from grams to tolas, from taels to ounces. Tolas and taels may sound exotic, while the measurements we use on a daily basis, grams and ounces, may seem mundane; however, that would be a misconception. The ounces that the gold market employs are not the standard avoirdupois ounces that we are used to in our daily lives. Instead these are *troy ounces*, a term thought to be derived from a precious metals market in the French town of Troies, which was held in medieval times.

It is the troy ounce that is referred to throughout this book (and in the market) as simply an ounce. This is the most important unit of measurement, with the global price of gold being quoted as a spread to the loco London price for a troy ounce of unallocated gold as part of a London Good Delivery bar. More practically referred to as just "loco London gold," this is discussed in detail in Chapter 3 on market making, where the exact meaning will be further elaborated. However, the basic definition of a London Good Delivery bar is core to the present chapter of this book.

Specifications for a London Good Delivery Gold Bar

The specifications for a London Good Delivery gold bar are laid out by the London Bullion Market Association (LBMA) on their Web site, www.lbma.org.uk. The LBMA describes itself on its site as "the trade association that acts as the coordinator for activities conducted on behalf of its members and other participants in the London bullion market. It acts as the principal point of contact between the market and its regulators."

The stringent testing needed before refineries are allowed accreditation as "Good Delivery refiners" ensures that standards are maintained and that those institutions that achieve this feat are regarded as producing metal that meets the minimum standards detailed herewith. Interestingly enough it is "strongly recommended" by the LBMA that the weight not be marked on each 400-ounce large bar because "when bars are weighed in London by an LBMA-approved weigher, their weights, which may be different, will prevail, and also any adjustment to the weight of a bar caused by future handling or sampling would necessitate alteration to the mark."

Basically, a London Good Delivery bar is the standard bar beloved of filmmakers when they are showing a heist from some impenetrable bank vault or another: films such as the *Italian Job* or *Three Kings*. Good Delivery bars are bars that weigh roughly 400 troy ounces each (about 12.5 kilograms), with a minimum gold content of 99.5 percent and (normally) with sloping sides to make them easier to handle. If you have ever tried to pick up one of these bars, it is much more difficult than it appears to be. Not only do they weigh considerably more than your brain tells you that they should, but also the metal can be somewhat slippery to the touch (although perhaps that is just from sweating palms!).

More formally, the LBMA sets the definitions as "The physical settlement of a loco London gold trade is a bar conforming to the following specifications:

Weight

- Minimum gold content: 350 fine troy ounces (approximately 10.9 kilograms)
- Maximum gold content: 430 fine troy ounces (approximately 13.4 kilograms)
- The gross weight of a bar should be expressed in troy ounces, in multiples of 0.025, rounded down to the nearest 0.025 of a troy ounce.

Dimensions

The recommended dimensions for a Good Delivery gold bar are approximately as follows:

- Length (Top): 250 mm +/− 40 mm Undercut*: 7% to 15%
- Width (Top): 70 mm +/− 15 mm Undercut[1]: 15% to 30%
- Height: 35 mm +/− 10 mm

---

*"Undercut" refers to the degree of slope on the side and ends of the bar and is calculated by deducting the dimension of the bottom edge of the bar from the dimension of the top edge and dividing the result by the top edge dimension multiplied by one hundred to obtain the percentage undercut.

Fineness

- The minimum acceptable fineness is 995.0 parts per thousand fine gold."

- Additionally, each bar has to have a serial number, the stamp of the refiner, year of manufacture, and the fineness of gold to four significant figures.

All of this may beg the question as to why London Good Delivery Bars are so important. The simple answer is that the stringent testing that the accredited refiners have to go through before their bars can be accepted as LGD gives the buyer confidence that the purity, in particular, is accurate. This holds true for smaller bars as well as for bars where both the weight and fineness are normally printed on the bar. Obviously these bars cannot be London Good Delivery because of their size, but the consumer can take some comfort if they have been produced by an accredited refiner. Indeed, some Asian and Middle Eastern buyers of gold bars will pay a premium for particular brands that they favor.

Large or Small Bars?

For refiners, their preference is generally to create smaller high value bars since their profit margins are slightly greater in what is a very competitive, low profit margin, business. The demand for physical gold can generally be judged by the premiums that can be charged for these smaller bars.

For example, if markups are high, then the refinery will gear its production toward small bars and will ship four nines (9999 or 99.99 percent pure) kilo bars to Hong Kong. If markups are low, or even at a discount to the loco London price, the refinery will have to sell its product as large bars (995 purity and known as "two nines five") into the international gold market. Often this means simply offering it on the London gold fixing.

Gold Miners and Hedging

·⊲⦙ Why Hedge? ⦙⊳·

 It is a myth, I hope, of the gold market that one of the very first hedges done was by an Australian mining company that was impressed that a bank was prepared to buy the gold that they were due to produce in five years at the same price as the current market. Obviously this overlooked the fact that gold is a contango market (so called because the forward curve is upward sloping). Such a trade, if true, would have an enormous profit for the bank involved.

Indeed it is this notion of contango that is central to gold hedging.

So what is contango?

·⊲⦙ Contango ⦙⊳·

For many commodities the natural shape of the price curve is backwardation, i.e., the price curve is downward sloping so that the higher price for nearby delivery, over longer term, reflects convenience yield, the need to have the material readily available (for industrial usage), and the fact that there may only be stockpiles available to last a few days or weeks so that the higher nearby price reflects the relative scarcity of the commodity.

I have read on a number of occasions that since gold prices are upward sloping with time, rather than involving a backwardation, then gold is actually in forwardation. To me *forwardation* is a word bandied about by individuals with little experience of the gold market, and indeed, I have never heard it used in a dealing room. Instead the term *contango* is universally adopted by traders.

As a more concrete example: if a gold mining company were to sell me spot gold (delivery in two business days time), then I would pay them $975 per ounce on the basis of current market prices. If that same producer wanted to sell me gold but not deliver it for 10 years, then I would pay them over $1,400 per ounce.

The calculation itself is simple, as shown in this example:

Spot gold (XAU) = $975

Gold forward rate (GOFO) = 4.50%

Days (t) = 3,652 (number of days between spot and delivery date)

The formula is also simple:

$$\text{10-year gold} = \text{XAU} + (((\text{XAU} \times \text{GOFO})/360) \times t)$$
$$= \$975 + \$445.088$$
$$= \$1,420.088$$

Incidentally, when gold prices are rolled forward, then it is market convention to use three decimal places for the price. So for deferred delivery there is the seductive prospect of a premium of $445 over the spot price; spot gold is delivered in London and New York two business days after the deal is transacted to allow for delivery of U.S. dollars (in New York) and gold (in London). Surely then it makes sense for companies to hedge at least a portion of their output in future years to protect cash flow and ensure the survival of the mine company?

The notion of contango makes virtually every financial instrument look attractive to the hedger. This is because option pricing models look at the forward price (which includes interest and holding costs, etc.) and determine how far away the strike price is from the notional forward price as one measure of the cost of the option. Using the example above, a mining company may believe that the current gold price of $975 represents a figure at which it is happy to sell metal over the longer term. The option model tells the miner that the cost of this protection for 10 years, buying a put, is $95 per ounce. Is it a price worth paying? Probably yes, when compared to the option struck at the forward price of $1,420, which would cost $255 per ounce.

In many instances, companies have decided that they would rather sell options to gain a premium rather than having to pay for them. Thus a mining company treasurer might have sold a $1,500 two-year gold call for $40, reasoning that the price is unlikely to rally by such a high percentage over the coming two years. However, there is the potential for problems to occur when there is a loss of control over who determines whether the option is exercised: the owner of the put or call—the miner in the first instance but the bank in the second. Thus, while $1,500 might seem an unachievable target over the next two years, financial graveyards are littered with the corpses of institutions that rationalized in such a way; the press singling out Long Term Capital Management as one of the most famous. So if hedging, then it makes sense to only hedge a portion of gold reserves, more perhaps for years in the near future than for those further out.

Clearly the argument about hedging is much more nuanced than can be set out in a book of this nature, both because strategies vary, but also because they are very dependent on the market's behavior thereafter. If the gold price were to rally strongly from today's levels, then those companies that have recently bought back outstanding hedges would be seen as prescient, whereas those who have been managing their books to ensure the least bad outcome would be seen as dilatory. However, should the converse occur, then the notion of "heroes" and "zeros" changes rapidly.

I think that probably the most eloquent argument in favor of hedging was made at a conference some years ago, when the chairman of a major mining company tried to demystify gold, arguing that a gold producer should act in much the same way as any other company.

To illustrate this he compared running a gold mine to owning a shoe shop. So protect cash flow and run your company as a normal business. Surely sound advice, except that there are many investors who buy equities in gold mining companies because they want exposure to the gold price. They believe that the mines are well managed and want to see gold prices rally. Conversely, it seems unlikely that anyone would buy shares in a shoe manufacturer in the expectation of the price of footwear going up.

In effect, there was a disconnect between the way in which some gold producers actually operated and the way in which a number of their shareholders wanted them to perform.

·⊰[Hedging]⊱·

During the 1990s, the heyday of forward selling, a rough rule of thumb was that Australian gold miners were the most hedged, followed by North Americans, with South Africans seen as relatively unhedged.

Even within countries practices varied wildly, with some Australian companies apparently hedging at 100 percent of forecast production, and some reputedly even in excess of this as they sought to prosper in the bear market that was gripping the industry. Tactics varied from selling far out of the money (or low delta) short-dated call options of a typical duration of one month or less to locking in the sale price of a proportion of mine production several years out, to 15 years in some instances.

The products themselves could vary from straightforward vanilla sales, to complex barrier options that would "knock-in" (or "out") if certain parameters were breached on certain dates or a series of dates. These products in turn might be linked to other areas of the producers' hedge book. This interdependence, fortunately not widespread, had great benefits for the treasurers of mining companies if prices remained low, but if gold rallied they might not only face having to sell metal at submarket prices but also having to pay a higher interest rate for the gold that they had borrowed. The notion of gold having an interest rate will be alien to some, but I will return to this topic in Chapter 4, where I discuss central banks and gold.

At its peak, it was estimated, by Virtual Metals Group and Haliburton Mineral Services, that the global market for gold sold before it had even been mined was 102.8 million ounces (3,212.50 tonnes). At the end of 2007 these organizations saw this figure to have fallen to just 26.8 million ounces or 837.5 tonnes. Some of these hedges will have rolled off, been allowed to mature, or will have had gold delivered into them, but a large percentage of this gold will have been bought back in the market.

So what changed? The short answer is the gold price, but as to why and whose fault it was that it got so low is a different matter. However, it was certainly an argument that rankled, and particularly during the 1990s when central banks and mining companies each accused the other, sometimes in private and sometimes publicly, of being to blame.

The Official Sector

·≈⟨ The Perception of Gold ⟩≈·

 A quick read of the media has probably assured most people not intimately acquainted with the gold market that central banks are keen buyers of the metal. Indeed much is being made of the fact that gold is the third "currency" behind the U.S. dollar and the euro and therefore these institutions need the metal as a constituent of their reserves: an essential part of any portfolio.

A quick roundup of some fairly recent remarks highlights this trend: "If we were the governor of the People's Bank of China or Reserve Bank of India or the Bank of Japan, we know what we would be doing: we would be quietly, but consistently, putting EUR and Dollar reserves on the offer and we would be, quietly and consistently, on the bid for gold." Thus wrote Dennis Gartman of the eponymous and influential newsletter in November 2005. Indeed this has been a recurrent theme of his and many other commentators.

In some instances the central banks have also been entering the debate. Consider the following: "China should appropriately increase its gold reserves and buy more oil, metals and other strategic materials so as to broaden the investment channels of the foreign exchange reserves."

Reuters reported these remarks as being made by Xiang Junbo, one of the deputy governors of the People's Bank of China (China's central bank).

The Russians probably elicited the most excitement when Maria Gueguina, head of Foreign Exchange Reserve Management at that country's central bank, said in a speech to the LBMA gold conference in Johannesburg (November 2005) that "Calculations of the Central Bank of Russia … showed that about 10 percent of gold in reserves would be appropriate with regard for special requirements." Given that the current percentage is just 2.5 percent, this would require the Russians to buy some 1,300 tonnes (41.6 million ounces). Although Ms. Gueguina subsequently clarified her remarks as being "theoretical" the price rallied strongly and particularly in the following few days as the same question was asked of other senior officials. The chairman of the central bank was quoted as saying that the gold "question is being discussed," and Reuters reported that "Russian President Vladimir Putin threw his weight behind the idea of boosting the share of gold in the central bank's fast-growing reserves." However, the quantities of gold held, reported by the Central Bank of Russia to the International Monetary Fund (IMF) have remained stable at 438 tonnes (the world's eleventh largest holder).

Generally though, it does not need a statement for analysts to speculate as to which country might be buying gold. All it needs is rapidly growing foreign exchange reserves and perhaps a poor relationship with the United States. The latter is often viewed as a requirement since it is assumed that these countries do not want to hold large quantities of dollars. Thus some of the countries that have been cited as buyers of gold, as they fit into at least one of the categories, are Saudi Arabia, Russia, India, Iran, Venezuela, South Africa, Brazil, etc.

·⊰[Holders of Gold]⊱·

Currently the world's largest holders of the metal, and the percentage it constitutes of their reserves, are shown in Table 4–1 (data as of March 2008):

The Official Sector

Table 4-1
World's Largest Holders of Gold

GLOBAL RANKING	COUNTRY	GOLD HOLDING (TONNES)	PERCENT RESERVES
1	United States	8,133.5	79.8%
2	Germany	3,417.4	68.9%
3	IMF	3,217.3	
4	France	2,586.9	59.7%
5	Italy	2,451.8	70.4%
6	Switzerland	1,133.9	42.9%
7	Japan	765.2	2.3%
8	The Netherlands	621.4	63.6%
9	China	600.0	1.1%
10	European Central Bank	563.6	26.7%

Source: © World Gold Council and IMF

A realistic appraisal of these figures shows that the world's largest holders of gold, certainly in percentage terms, are the "old economies" of the West with Asia represented by only China and Japan. However, their metal holdings are just tiny percentages of their overall reserves.

Taking a look at the Asian economies themselves it is simple to see just how little gold some of these institutions hold both as a percentage and simply numerically. So while the Asian nations listed in Table 4–2, on average, hold less than 3 percent of their reserves in gold, the figure for the European countries (Table 4–1) is over 50 percent.

Indeed, looking back on the statistics for movements in central bank gold holdings over the last 10 years, there is an enormous preponderance of minus signs. In other words sales of gold are the dominant feature of central banks' activity in the gold market. True there have been some purchases but these have tended to be relatively modest and often stem from a requirement that small-scale domestic miners

Table 4–2
Leading Asian Holders of Gold

WORLDWIDE RANKING	COUNTRY	GOLD HOLDING (TONNES)	PERCENT RESERVES
7	Japan	765.2	2.3%
9	China	600.0	1.1%
12	Taiwan	423.3	4.4%
14	India	357.7	3.6%
26	Singapore	127.4	2.2%
27	Philippines	127.4	11.0%
33	Thailand	84.0	2.7%
37	Indonesia	73.1	3.8%
45	Malaysia	36.4	1.0%
57	Korea	14.3	0.2%

Source: © World Gold Council and IMF

have to sell the metal to the central bank, which can either add the gold to its reserves or sell it into the international market.

The only real headline grabbers were the purchase by Poland of gold in the 1990s—assumed to have been bought from another European central bank—as well as the announcements by China that they had bought metal in 2002 and 2003, and finally the statement by Argentina in 2004 that it had purchased slightly under 30 tonnes of metal for reserve diversification.

With all due respect to Poland and Argentina, it is the Chinese purchase that is the most significant—indeed, given that they have previously bought gold, would they be likely to do so again, especially considering that gold purchases only constitute 1.1 percent of China's ever-growing foreign exchange reserves.

A little bit of history: In January 2002, China announced an increase in their gold reserves from 12.7 to 16.08 million ounces. The original figure, released to the IMF for the first time in the 1970s, had been unchanged until the press release. This increase occurred despite a law mandating the sale of the country's gold production to the central bank (People's Bank of China, also known as the PBoC). The PBoC then adjusted the domestic price to allow gold to flow into, or out of, the country. Almost exactly a year later, the figure rose again to 19.29 million ounces or roughly 602 tonnes. If such an announcement were to be made now, then it is likely that gold prices would move rapidly higher because traders would anticipate further purchases. However, the reaction at the time was considerably more subdued as analysts assumed that rather than being fresh purchases of the metal, the increases were more a restatement of balances actually held.

Indeed, the figures reported to the IMF are not independently audited, and thus there have been suggestions of both over- and underreporting by a number of countries.

ᴥ Buyers of Gold? ᴥ

Before asking who buys gold, it is worth examining why a central bank should hold gold in the first place. This inquiry would then lead to debate on diversification, gold being no one's debt, and an impression of tradition and solidity: the standard features attributed to gold.

Assuming that the diversification argument is generally the strongest, many central banks will classify their mission as the preservation of reserves by ensuring liquidity, a basically conservative approach. Central banks tend not to be wealth creators but rather are charged with maintaining a status quo—something that can be seen both as part of their charter as well as reflected in their remuneration, in which performance incentive payments are relatively rare. In this sense gold fits the requirements well. It is a traditional asset and one held by the majority of central banks.

Assuming that China, Russia, and India—countries that have been suggested as buyers of gold—decided to acquire more metal for diversification, then how much metal would this involve? A 1 percent holding of gold is clearly too little to count; the most recent large central bank to be inaugurated was the European Central Bank, which opted for 15 percent, although this amount is more related to the fact that the bank's members were almost all large holders of the metal in the first place, over 50 percent in some cases. So perhaps a figure of 10 percent might be appropriate, particularly given the theoretical remarks by Maria Gueguina of the Central Bank of Russia. This figure also has the advantage of being slightly over double the 3 to 5 percent that many institutions are seeking to invest in commodity markets: a new asset class rather than a traditional central bank staple.

Table 4–3

Theoretical Gold Purchases by the Central Banks of China, Russia, and India

COUNTRY	10 PERCENT GOLD HOLDING	CURRENT RESERVES	REQUIRED PURCHASE
China	5,450t	600.0t	4,850.0t
Russia	1,610t	450.9t	1,159.1t
India	995.0t	357.7t	637.3t

t = tonnes

By this very rough measure, for just these three institutions to hold 10 percent of their reserves in gold they would have to purchase 6,646 tonnes. This is equivalent to over 2 1/2 years of global gold production. To put this into perspective, under the selling agreement reached by the European central banks, the signatories are limited to selling 500 tonnes of gold between them per annum—this figure being seen as a quantity that should not unduly disrupt the market. Adopting the same logic, it would take over 13 years for these three institutions to reach their target, by which time their reserves would doubtless have grown substantially.

If the percentage were to be 3 percent, then it would still be an enormous figure, but this time the story is centered almost entirely on China, which would have to buy over 1,000 tonnes. More generally though, the problem that central banks have had with gold is its high profile. If a central bank opts to increase the percentage of euros it holds in its reserves at the expense of U.S. dollars, then that is a short-lived headline for the financial markets. If this same central bank were to start selling its gold holdings, then this often would presage a press campaign fixated on some form of family heirloom being disposed of in an under-handed way. In 1999, when Gordon Brown was chancellor of the exchequer, minister of finance, for the United Kingdom, he opted to sell 395 tonnes of the country's gold reserves at an approximate average price per tonne of $275—a decision that is still recalled whenever his opponents wish to question his financial competence.

This situation exemplifies the dilemma that gold presents for the official sector: that gold has been a buy-and-hold investment. Once owned, gold is extremely difficult to dispose of. A fitting metaphor is that of the lobster trap—it's very tempting to enter but next to impos-sible to exit. Nevertheless I see two possibilities for state entities to buy significant quantities of gold, the first being in something of an auto-cratic country where the central bank is instructed to accumulate gold. The second is via sovereign wealth funds (SWFs), in which a nation would simply treat the investment as an unannounced trading position—in effect, a radical departure from the sort of activities that we have seen from countries in the past—so that the gold could be sold again at the appropriate time. Current estimates are that the SWFs have some $3 trillion under management, and again even a few percentage points of investment would translate to an enormous investment in this market—each percentage point accounting for over 900 tonnes (on a basis of $1,000 per ounce).

Many people would disagree with me and instead point to the possibility of an "off market" transaction. For example, I have seen suggestions that China, Saudi Arabia, and others would not buy in the market, but instead would simply hold high-level negotiations with their equivalents at a European central bank. The governors of the two institutions would agree on a market-neutral price, and then gold would change hands on the basis of the gold fixing, as a bench-mark on a certain day or on the average over a period of time. Indeed, this might seem to be a persuasive argument that attends to the needs of both parties. However, I am rather more cynical.

For the seller, the central bank is keen to reassure its population that it has achieved the best possible price. It has to avoid accusations that it sold the metal inappropriately or too cheaply, as mentioned previously, a consistent charge leveled at UK prime minister Gordon Brown, although the UK is a slightly different case in that the gold reserves belong to the government rather than to the central bank.

In other nations it is equally complicated, where the governor of the central bank does not want to see either the office or the institution criticized in the legislature for economic mismanagement. Thus in most situations gold is sold over an extended period of time to present an appropriate average. Theoretically then, it would still be possible for China to buy gold from France or another European nation. However—and it is a large however—any news that an Asian nation, oil-producing state, or sovereign wealth fund had bought significant quantities of gold would cause an immediate upward spike in the gold price. Statements that this was the only purchase would be ignored. Instead traders would focus both on the likelihood that this counterpart would buy more gold and that others would look to replicate this trade.

Therefore, far from being viewed as off-market sellers achieving a market-neutral price, they would be judged as having sold significantly below the market, with the commensurate political fallout. I said above that this was a cynical view, but I know of at least one central bank that has had precisely this debate, in these terms, of whether to try to find a buyer or to sell the gold into the market. That central bank opted for the latter, political, solution.

Perhaps the situation for the IMF might be different. Currently the IMF is debating sales, and given that the gold is theoretically owned by several nations, perhaps an agreement could be reached. However, I am far from convinced.

The selling agreement entered into by the European central banks introduced above forms the basis of the next section of this chapter.

⊸[Central Banks Selling Gold]⊶

For much of the 1990s gold was in an unremitting bear market. It was seen as an antiquated investment whose time had passed in favor of a new era of financial engineering and the dot-com boom. As mentioned in Chapter 3, regarding the activities of gold producers, in many instances they were selling gold that they had yet to mine to protect the future of their operations, and speculators were short-selling gold in a version of the yen "carry trade"—whereby essentially hedge funds and others would sell gold, borrow it back at the low gold interest rate, and then invest the dollars from their sales in high-yielding instruments (or even in Treasury bills). The fact that gold was slipping lower meant that not only were speculators gaining on the yield, but they were also enjoying a capital appreciation as the price of the metal kept on falling.

Rightly, many central banks were unwilling to simply watch as gold fell ever lower and the national wealth evaporated. Toward the end of the decade, we had seen the Belgians, Dutch, and Canadians, along with other nations, selling gold. The nadir came when, during the course of 1999, a number of nations who were thought to be friendly to the metal sought to lighten up on their holdings.

The Australians sold, and the United Kingdom and Switzerland both declared their intention to divest roughly half of their holdings; the Swiss divested a rather more material 1,300 tonnes compared to the UK's 395 tonnes.

The market had, to a certain extent, gotten used to the idea that central banks sell gold. Investors did not care for this idea, but it was accepted. However, when news of the Australian sale broke, the market was caught totally off guard. The fact that the press release seemed to suggest that the Reserve Bank of Australia and the government had decided on this course of action because the country had plenty of metal in the ground did little to satisfy the detractors. The mining companies were particularly unimpressed and pointed out that the unmined gold belonged to them rather than to the government—adding insult to injury, the announcement caused the gold price to sink further.

In the same way, it was assumed that the Swiss had some sort of affinity for gold, that it was as much a part of their culture as chocolate and banking. However, this was not the case. In a similar fashion London is generally seen as the home of the gold market, with the majority of metal around the world trading loco London, where the benchmark gold price (the fixing) is determined, and furthermore it is also home to many of the largest global market-makers and the place where the rules defining the industry standard, the "London Good Delivery bar," are set. The United Kingdom was a long-term holder of gold. In the same way as with the Swiss, the market had been rather too complacent, and the UK government, who actually own the UK's reserves (unlike the situation in most other countries where it belongs to the central bank), were indeed sellers and preferred to hold the euro.

The unexpected actions of these three countries in particular gave many investors the impression that all central banks were queuing up to sell gold, that it was far more a question of when every holder sold rather than "if." The fact that three countries that had been considered to be "friendly" to gold were all selling gave rise to the suspicion that the outlook was so bearish that countries were leapfrogging each other in their eagerness to sell.

Gold plumbed 19-year lows during 1999, falling to $252, with some mining companies accusing the central banks of not only distorting the gold market by selling but also helping hedge funds—who borrowed gold to fund their carry trades—to push the price lower. The rejoinder from the official sector was simple and to the point; they felt that it was the producers whose hedging policies were to blame, that "accelerated selling" was the real destroyer of value. One memorable rejoinder I heard from a senior central banker was: "At least we are selling gold that we already have; not something that might not even be dug up for 10 years."

On September 26, 1999 the situation changed dramatically.

⟶ European central bank Gold Agreement ⟵

The heading "European central bank Gold Agreement" might look like a weird mixture of upper and lower case letters, a typographical error, but the agreement is normally referred to as EcbGA, although sometimes also as WAG, the Washington Agreement on Gold. This jumble of letters was to underline the scope of the agreement while seeking to make clear that this was not simply a declaration by the European Central Bank (thus giving all capitals) but to make clear that a number of European central banks were involved.

On Monday September 27, 1999 I was working in Sydney. Given the time difference, it was a Sunday and a day earlier when Wim Duisenberg (the then president of the European Central Bank) issued a statement on behalf of 15 central banks in Washington.

These 15 banks were the central banks of the United Kingdom, Switzerland, Sweden, and the ECB, plus the Euroland 11—namely, Germany, France, Italy, the Netherlands, Portugal, Spain, Austria, Belgium, Luxembourg, Finland, and Ireland.

⟶ EcbGA–Mark I ⟵

1. Gold will remain an important element of global monetary reserves.

2. The above institutions will not enter the market as sellers, with the exception of already decided sales.

3. Gold sales already decided will be achieved through a concerted programme of sales over the next five years. Annual sales will not exceed approximately 400 tonnes and total sales over this period will not exceed 2,000 tonnes.

4. The signatories to this agreement have agreed not to expand their gold leasings and their use of gold futures and options over this period.

5. This agreement will be reviewed after five years.

The initial reaction was one of caution. Everyone knew it was important, but what should the gold price do? It had closed on Friday night at around $267 in New York, and from there it started to creep up slowly. Bizarre as it might seem now, much of the market's attention initially focused on the impact to the gold lending market, where there were already concerns over Y2K plus liquidity over the turn of the year and the millennium. I called all the clients in my address book and woke people up from Europe to the United States. Again there were few buyers, but everyone wanted to be kept "in touch."

The media had no such reservations. Instead, newswires and newspapers were full of articles trumpeting the restraint of the central banks, despite the fact that the total of 2,000 tonnes to be sold over five years was more than double the sales from these countries over the previous 10 years. The result was that gold rallied to $338 over the course of the next few days—a gain of some 26 percent. Gold interest rates soared too, with one-month rates reaching a high of 10 percent from 4 percent just a few days earlier.

As the metal's price started to spike, gold mining companies started to make announcements of their own. One of the first was Ghana's Ashanti Goldfields, which announced that it had restructured 80 percent of its hedge-book, converting "forward sale positions into synthetic (put) options." Technically this restructuring would have involved them buying call options with the same strike and expiry as the existing sales. Clearly this looked to be a smart move until October 5, 1999, when they announced that the hedge-book had a negative value of some $450 million. Subsequently Ashanti announced that it had entered into a standstill agreement with its 16 bank counterparts, which had agreed not to request further margin calls. The company was ultimately taken over by AngloGold in April 2004 to form AngloGold Ashanti.

Similarly, Cambior Inc. of Canada announced that they were in discussions with banks "to determine … the manner and sequence in which Cambior's gold delivery obligations will be met."

The fact that the gold price could rally but companies that mine gold might still lose money was not a prospect that had probably ever occurred to investors.

However, just three months later, almost all these gains had been given back—despite the predictions of doom as the world approached New Year's Eve 1999—with spot gold back at $274 and one-month gold deposits only paying 1.5 percent.

The Producers

While governments and their related institutions can enter into agreements to regulate supply, the same leeway cannot be extended to individuals or typical companies. Think of OPEC or indeed the signatories to EcbGA. However, for companies the accusations would be of antitrust and cartels, with the consequent potential for enormous damages from class-action lawsuits. Thus there was no chance that they could respond formally, as a group, to the statement from the central banks.

However, in early 2000 a number of press releases were issued by individual producers. All were basically to the effect that they would rein back their hedging, also known as accelerated supply. In February 2000, Placer Dome (then the third-largest North American gold mining company) announced: "As of this day, the company has ceased adding any new hedge positions" and "We believe that gold prices will move higher. The agreement by European central banks to limit their sales and lending was an important step toward improving market sentiment, but industry needs to do its part."

Ultimately, it was the formal statement by the 15 central banks and the impact that it had on the activities of individual mining companies that allowed the recent rally in gold to all-time highs to take place. Simply put, it removed uncertainty and allowed positive sentiment to flourish.

⋅≺[EcbGA—Mark II]≻⋅

The original agreement was so influential that almost immediately rumors emerged that it would be abrogated. These rumors were rapidly followed by conjecture as to whether it would be renewed. Both of these stories were avidly reported in the financial press, but in my view there was never any question that the central banks would not closely follow the strictures that they themselves had set. Any suggestion that they were "bending the rules" would undoubtedly have impacted the reputation of central banks for many years to come and made their lives far harder in markets where it is vital that their pronouncements are taken at face value (setting interest rates for example).

The rumors were dispelled six months earlier, on March 8, 2004, when the following statement appeared on the Web site of the ECB (www.ecb.int):

> In the interests of clarifying their intentions with respect to their gold holdings, the undersigned institutions make the following statement:
>
> 1. Gold will remain an important element of global monetary reserves.
>
> 2. The gold sales already decided and yet to be decided by the undersigned institutions will be achieved through a concerted programme of sales over a period of 5 years, starting on the 27th September 2004, just after the end of the previous agreement. Annual sales will not exceed 500 tonnes and total sales over this period will not exceed 2,500 tonnes.
>
> 3. Over this period, the signatories to this agreement have agreed that the total amount of gold leasings and the total amount of their use of gold futures and options will not exceed the amounts prevailing at the date of the signature of the previous agreement.
>
> 4. This agreement will be reviewed after five years.

This time the signatories were the European Central Bank, Banco de Espana (Spain), Bank of Greece, Banque de France, Central Bank and Financial Services Authority of Ireland, De Nederlandsche Bank (The Netherlands), Oesterreichisch Nationalbank (Austria), Schweitzerische

Nationalbank (Switzerland), Banca d'Italia (Italy), Banco de Portugal, Banque Nationale de Belgique (Belgium), Deutsche Bundesbank (Germany), Suomen Pankki (Finland), and Sveriges Riksbank (Sweden).

At the time of signing these institutions had combined gold holdings of approximately 13,900 tonnes, which equated to around 40 percent of all gold then held by the official sector.

Since the announcement was made, the original signatories have been joined by the central banks of Slovenia, Malta, and Cyprus. The latter pair were the most recent, signing up on January 25, 2008.

Mark I Versus Mark II

The most significant change is that the tonnage of sales was increased from 2,000 tonnes over five years up to 2,500 tonnes, an increase in allowable sales of 100 tonnes per annum. The amount was judged by the central banks as one not to cause any market disruption and was arrived at after considerable informal consultation with the largest gold trading banks. It remains the maximum amount that can be sold in any quota year (September 27 to September 26) rather than a target. Thus the full year allowable amount does not need to be filled—an important consideration and one that has helped the recent rally in the gold price. Unwritten in the agreement is that the original EcbGA was about returning stability to the gold market. Indeed I know there was debate, originally and subsequently, about the first tenet that "Gold will remain an important element of global monetary reserves"; in many ways an odd remark from institutions who were embarking on selling it but important as a message to help sentiment.

Therefore, while central banks are allowed to roll any gold sales forward there has been a conscious effort to ensure that the settlement date of the transactions falls within the relevant quota year. Similarly, central banks have been involved in the options market, tending to sell call options. These options have generally been assumed to be 100 percent delta, i.e., the options are accounted for at full face value until they expire rather than the values suggested by the option pricing models, again to ensure that they are complying with the spirit of the accord.

While both agreements were originally signed by 15 countries, in Mark II Greece took the place of the Bank of England. The rationale given by the Bank of England for not participating was that "The UK government has no plans to sell holdings of gold from its reserves and will therefore not participate in the renewal of the Agreement on Gold announced by European Central Banks today.

The Government remains firmly committed to transparency and ensuring the integrity of the gold market. Consequently an announcement will be made if the UK's policy on gold sales changes in the future."

All perfectly logical, except that cynics pointed out that some other signatories were also extremely unlikely to sell gold as they had such small balances, in particular pointing to Ireland (5.5 tonnes) and Luxembourg (2.3 tonnes). However, the concerns of the conspiracy theorists have not been borne out.

EcbGA–Mark III?

If the European central banks intend to adhere to their timing then we should know by March 2009 whether there is likely to be a further five-year extension. Indeed I had a number of central banks ask my opinion as early as March 2008—a full year in advance or even 18 months from the end of the previous agreement—as to whether another accord was necessary. My perception is that these institutions, in common with all of us, do not like to be restricted and would be far happier to have freedom of action. Therefore their preference would be merely to note that gold has recently reached all-time nominal highs and therefore there is no need for a further agreement. They could also note that the rationale for the original agreement was to provide stability and certainty to a market beset by rumor and pessimism—in this their original action accomplished its purpose extremely well.

However, my response to these central banks has been that gold is very much a sentiment-driven market. Thus while the current market could probably shrug off the lack of EcbGA Mark III, it is by no means assured that the same would be true at a later date. Therefore, given that markets generally like certainty, it would be preferable if the accord were to be renewed for a further term. A renewal would be particularly important should the IMF be successful in its quest to sell gold.

·◦⟨ The IMF and Gold ⟩◦·

Under the charter of the International Monetary Fund, the organization is allowed to hold gold or to sell it. There is no middle ground as there is for most official institutions, which can at least attempt to earn a return by lending their gold. So the gold just sits on their balance sheet but serves very little purpose.

The IMF has previously sold gold, through a series of successful auctions during the 1970s. The recent discussions really began in earnest during the late 1990s, when then British Prime Minister Tony Blair suggested that the IMF sell gold to assist the Heavily Indebted Poor Countries (HIPC). While this had some support, it was also roundly condemned by more vociferous voices. The complaints were generally:

1. It is not the IMF's gold to dispose of as it wishes; instead, it belongs to the countries that originally granted it to them. Therefore if the IMF has no further use for its gold, it should simply hand it back to the original donors.

2. The IMF is an inefficient and bureaucratic organization, and it should first get its own finances in order before dispensing largesse.

3. Most tellingly though, several African nations with mining industries lined up to condemn the proposals. They cited increased gold sales as damaging to the very nations that the disposal was supposed to help.

Unsurprisingly, the idea was dropped, although there were a series of one-off "accounting tricks" that allowed the IMF to value gold at market prices. The IMF provides this account on its Web site:

"Between December 1999 and April 2000, separate but closely linked transactions involving a total of 12.9 million ounces of gold were carried out between the IMF and two members (Brazil and Mexico) that had financial obligations falling due to the IMF. In the first step, the IMF sold gold to the member at the prevailing market price, and the profits were placed in a special account invested for the benefit of the HIPC Initiative. In the second step, the IMF immediately accepted back, at the same market price, the same amount of gold from the member in settlement of that member's financial obligations. The net effect of these transactions was to leave the balance of the IMF's holdings of physical gold unchanged." (For further details, see http://www.imf.org/external/np/exr/facts/gold.htm.)

For the market, the situation remained unchanged until January 2007, with the emergence of the "eminent persons" report on gold sales. This time it was clear that the IMF had sought to forestall the type of criticism that it had faced before. Also, the notion of helping the HIPC had been dropped in favor of sales settling the IMF's financing needs.

This report marked a major departure from the political "kite-flying" that we saw previously. This time attempts were made to address the majority of the criticisms that might be leveled at it. Importantly, the persons who actually put their name to the report were of sufficient stature to dispel most doubts that this was a serious proposal.

First, the commission included Tito Mboweni, governor of the South African Reserve Bank. South Africa was a vocal critic of the original proposals, some 10 years ago, for the IMF to sell gold, arguing that it would actually harm the Heavily Indebted Poor Countries that it was supposed to help. On subsequent occasions, South Africa has toned down its displeasure, and now it is firmly aligned with the sellers. Indeed, the chairman went out of his way at a press conference to emphasize that South Africa was part of the group and that the committee "has been quite careful to try to devise proposals that do not create dangers of destabilizing the gold market." (See further at http://www.imf.org/external/np/tr/2007/tr070131.htm.)

Also present on the "Eminent Persons Group" was Jean-Claude Trichet. As president of the ECB, he would obviously be able to secure a quota under the EcbGA; after all, it was brokered by his own organization. This would allow the IMF, and the central banks, to argue that the sales were not adding to market expectations of supply, the inference being that the German quota argued for under Bundesbank President Ernst Welteke (and seemingly not required by his successor Axel Weber) was to be given to the IMF. In effect should the approval be rapid, then EcbGA Mark II would be close to hitting its overall limit of 2,500 tonnes.

In a sense they are absolutely correct—except that the market has grown used to the idea that there was to be a massive shortfall due to Germany's reluctance to sell (a dispute between the central bank and the government as to who would receive the proceeds). The "scorecard" so far has been the maximum of 500 tonnes per annum being hit in 2004/2005, a shortfall of over 100 tonnes in 2005/2006, and a small miss of roughly 13 tonnes in 2006/2007. While the signatories have not said what each country's quota actually is, the "guess" from the market has been that other central banks were willing to accelerate their sales, with the result that the final year of the agreement (September 27, 2008 to September 26, 2009) would be significantly below 500 tonnes in the absence of any selling from Germany. It is into this space that first the Swiss, with their increased selling, and now seemingly the IMF are looking to step.

If the tone of the gold market can remain positive and generally supportive, then traders can probably shrug this off if the sales are carried out in a sensitive manner.

Interestingly, the governors of both the Saudi Arabian Monetary Agency and the People's Bank of China were also on the panel. These countries have been cited repeatedly by many analysts as two organizations likely to buy gold. The significance of this could be argued on two counts: first, that terms of an off-market sale have already been agreed upon, and that the presence of both these gentlemen is a tacit acknowledgment of this.

Secondly, however, we have previously heard from the IMF that their efforts to find a buyer for a portion of their gold proved to be impossible. If Saudi Arabia or China were in the market for a substantial amount of gold, then presumably this notion of a direct sale to a central bank could just have been floated again. The fact that it appears likely that any gold sale will be accounted for under EcbGA tends to reduce the likelihood of an off-market sale. In addition, there is my earlier point, that a private transaction tends to favor the buyer. I cannot see the IMF wanting to put itself in a position where its critics can point to financial mismanagement—a charge almost certain to be leveled at it should the price rally sharply subsequent to any sale.

The proposal still has to be voted on by the members of the IMF to proceed. Under the charter, any gold sales will require an 85 percent approval level; given that the votes are weighted according to the input of the original donors, the United States has 17 percent of the votes. In other words this constitutes an effective veto should it decide to block progress.

It seems likely, though, that between the committee chairman (Andrew Crockett, ex-BIS and president of JPMorgan Chase International) and "eminent person" Alan Greenspan, there would be a good understanding of the likelihood of this proposal being passed by Congress. Indeed, almost exactly a year later, in February 2008, the U.S. Treasury's undersecretary for international affairs, David McCormick, announced that he was in favor of gold sales and that he believed the proposal would be passed by the U.S. Congress.

In April 2008, Dominique Strauss-Kahn, managing director of the IMF, was able to announce that the institution had agreed to sell 403.3 tonnes of gold, which would be used to create an endowment: "We have made difficult but necessary choices to close the projected income shortfall and put the fund's finances on a sustainable basis, but in the end it will make the fund more focused, efficient, and cost-effective in serving the needs of our members" (see http://www.imf. org/external/np/sec/pr/2008/pr0874.htm). The sale still needs to be approved by all 185 members of the IMF, but it seems likely that it will pass, given the apparent goodwill from all sides on this occasion. Assuming that it goes ahead, the funds are earmarked for government bonds in the first instance followed by corporate bonds at some unspecified date in the future and even by equities.

On their Web site, the organization states that their "policy on gold is governed by the following principles:

- As an undervalued asset held by the IMF, gold provides fundamental strength to its balance sheet. Any mobilization of IMF gold should avoid weakening its overall financial position.

- The IMF should continue to hold a relatively large amount of gold among its assets, not only for prudential reasons, but also to meet unforeseen contingencies.

- The IMF has a systemic responsibility to avoid causing disruptions to the functioning of the gold market.

- Profits from any gold sales should be used whenever feasible to create an investment fund, of which only the income should be used."

For further details, see http://www.imf.org/external/np/exr/facts/gold.htm.

While the IMF is something of a special case, not being allowed to lend their gold, this still neatly illustrates the dilemma even for the many institutions that can lend gold. The market is simply too small, and yields are extremely low, to lend a country's entire reserves, and thus there is a major gap between the nominal size of a central bank's foreign exchange reserves and those that actually earn a yield. Gold is traditionally a "buy and hold" reserve, but for many institutions they are increasingly being judged on effective management of their holdings; thus the rational decision could be seen to reduce gold reserves and buy an asset that yields a return. It certainly argues against holding/buying large quantities of gold (in percentage terms).

I know of several instances where central banks are charged with managing their reserves—the profits are used first to pay for the upkeep of the institution (including salaries) with the excess being remitted to the government—but given the high percentages of gold held and the low yield they are now unable to meet their running costs. The result is that the central bank now has to go to the ministry of finance for funds to keep operating. Politically this is very unpopular and has been behind the sales decision of some of the sellers.

·≈[Selling—Keeping the Score]≈·

The simple answer is that keeping the score is a lot less easy than some analysts try to make out.

Every Tuesday there is a press release from the European Central Bank at 3 p.m. Frankfurt time, which generally equates to 2 p.m. in London and 9 a.m. in New York. This is the consolidated weekly financial statement of the Eurosystem and shows changes in the overall balance sheet of its members. At the end of each quarter, the data is released one day later, on a Wednesday.

The first problem with this information is that it does not include nations that have signed the gold agreement but are not members of the euro, Switzerland clearly being the most prominent example. Second, I get very bored with endless news reports telling me that the announcement for the decline in members' gold reserves (expressed in euros) is the quantity of gold that was sold the previous week. It is not—it is merely the difference in the balance sheet: a simple expression of accounting changes. Thus what it actually shows is sales that settled that week. In other words, if a central bank were to sell 10 tonnes of gold and roll it forward for six months, then this transaction would be captured in the ECB's data in six months' time but not next week.

So while it is vaguely useful as a method of keeping score, it is generally irrelevant, particularly so in the early stages of a "quota year." However, once we begin to approach September (each quota year ends on September 26), then the cumulative total has more relevance—if it is considerably less than the year's allocation, then the market can generally take some comfort since it is unlikely that all the gold would either be sold in the final few months or indeed rolled to that date. Therefore, this is normally seen as a bullish signal.

Lenders and Borrowers of Gold

·=][Who Lends and Borrows Gold?]c·

 The previous chapter was concerned with central banks adding to and/or decreasing their gold holdings. However, the normal activities of countries are far more mundane and less noteworthy.

Generally the managers of a country's wealth seek to maximize the yield of their reserves. In many cases, their role is to handle these reserves efficiently with profits generated to be used for the upkeep of the central bank and any additional to be remitted to the ministry of finance. I must stress that this is by no means true in all countries, but it is a reasonable generalization.

Despite the oft-repeated refrain that "gold has no yield," this is simply not always true, although it may well be for small holdings. In fact, gold does have an interest market comparable to other financial instruments. True, that market is much smaller, but it does exist. The other feature that makes it different is the absence of a central authority directing policy and trying to set rates. Instead, the market is determined purely by supply and demand: the former overwhelmingly from central banks (over 90 percent), while the latter was traditionally seen as gold producers (around 70 percent), physical consignment stocks (around 15 percent), and market shorts making up the balance.

During the 1990s, when producer hedging was at its peak, it was generally estimated that around 4,500 tonnes of gold was lent to the market by central banks before peaking at 4,940 tonnes (according to an estimate from the Virtual Metals Group) toward the end of 2000, roughly one-sixth of total holdings. Some theorists speculated that up to four times as much metal could have been lent as part of a conspiracy to depress the price of gold. One of the outlandish theories was that Germany had lent their entire gold reserves to the Clinton administration in an ultimately unsuccessful attempt to keep the price low (more on this in Chapter 10, "Gold: Myths and Reality").

At this time it was not uncommon for rates to spike as rumors of central bank withdrawals of gold from the market caused some of the less credit-worthy bullion banks to become concerned that they would not be able to source sufficient material to service their loan books. In many cases the model adopted by some institutions was to lend gold on a long-dated basis (for up to 10 or even 15 years) to mining companies (which were funding their hedge books) while borrowing metal from central banks, or the market, which might only be prepared to lend metal for less than six months. However, the gold interest rate curve was so steep that this practice was deemed an acceptable risk.

·⊰[The Yield Curve]⊱·

The shape of the yield curve has changed little over the years, as can be seen from Figure 5–1, with the line unsurprisingly sloping upward from 1 to 10 years. What has changed, though, is that over the last few years, the entire curve, and hence the yield, has fallen each year.

Since gold interest rates are determined purely by supply and demand—rather than by a central authority—then it is clear that one of these dynamics has changed. In this instance it is the borrowing interest

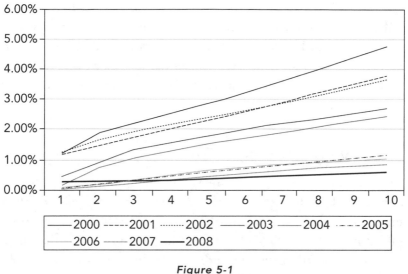

Figure 5-1

The Yield Curve

(from mining companies) that has dried up. This rationale is covered in a little more depth in Chapter 3, "Gold Miners and Hedging."

As mentioned above, producers were the vast majority of the borrowers of gold for use in their hedging programs. Considering that the global hedgebook was estimated as 3,212.50 tonnes (Virtual Metals Group and Haliburton Mineral Services) at its peak against 4,940 tonnes of gold being lent, then it is reasonably simple to see the influence of this accelerated selling, although the figures are a little overinflated due to the inclusion of options in the overall total.

Because miners were looking to take advantage of the contango in the gold price (contango is discussed in Chapter 3, but basically it is defined as the upward sloping price of gold over time) and to protect long-dated cash flows, their interest was to transact at the long end of the curve; in some instances as far out as 15 years. They hedged this exposure to gold interest rates both by locking in long-term rates and by rolling a series of short-term floating ones, three months for example.

It was clearly much more expensive initially to pay for certainty rather than be exposed to the vagaries of market moves. Consequently, the miners tended to fix only a very small proportion of their long-term gold borrowing preferring to manage their risk via a series of short-term borrows—anything generally from one to six months where there was the greatest liquidity.

·◦] Paying Interest in Gold or U.S. Dollars? [◦·

The chart in Figure 5–1 shows the yield in U.S. dollars—expressed in percent—of a gold deposit. A bullet rate of interest is paid in full at maturity rather than semiannually, etc. This is a crucial distinction; in fact in the early 1990s some institutions did not realize that there was a significant difference for interest rates that paid a return in gold or in U.S. dollars.

The rationale is reasonably simple. If the borrowers and lenders agree that interest should be paid at maturity in U.S. dollars, then the value of the deposit and/or loan is calculated with respect to the spot price. In other words, the interest is the amount of gold multiplied by the spot price.

If the interest is to be paid in gold, and the interest rate is the same, then at maturity the lender will get back the original principal in full plus interest, i.e., one ounce of gold or $975 (which was equivalent to the original spot price) to be paid at maturity. If lenders know that they will receive one ounce of gold in 10 years time, then they could forward-sell it instead. Because gold is a contango market, they would end up receiving considerably more than $975 for it—in fact they would receive $1,420 for that ounce. This difference clearly explains why interest rates that are payable in gold (known as "gold in gold") are different from those in which interest is payable in dollars (gold in dollars).

In the current environment of low interest rates, it generally makes a difference of a few basis points if any at all, and only then in longer term rates, but previously it was a significant factor.

It is worth noting though that almost all gold deposits have interest payable in U.S. dollars, which is at the request of the lenders—the central banks.

The following section should clarify this topic.

⇥ Calculating Interest on Gold ⇤

The types of trade entered into by the central banks were generally fairly vanilla, and most often were gold "leases" or "deposits." These two terms do not necessarily denote the same thing, but lazy market jargon uses them interchangeably.

A lease is no different from a money market deposit. In other words, the lender places gold with a bank in return for payment of interest. To clear up a common misconception, if a bank is lent gold, this does not mean that it then has to sell gold and place the dollars gained on deposit. Gold has its own interest rate market, and thus it would be akin to suggesting that should a lender place euros, sterling, yen, etc. on deposit, then the borrower needs to enter the foreign exchange market to sell each currency to generate dollars, which are then lent for the interest. This scenario is clearly nonsense; however, the notion was fairly widespread and helped extend the proliferation of conspiracy theories.

One example is a 12-month gold deposit:

The lender places 100,000 troy ounces on deposit for 12 months at 20 basis points.

At maturity, the central bank has returned to it the 100,000 ounces of gold plus the accrued interest of 202.778 ounces.

The calculation is simple:

$$((100,000 \times 0.20\%)/360) \times 365 = 202.778 \text{ ounces.}$$

The day count convention is referred to as "actual over 360."

Most lenders, though, prefer to accumulate interest in U.S. dollars. In which case, a monetary value is ascribed to gold at the outset of the trade, and the calculation becomes:

$$(($975 \times 100,000 \times 0.20\%)/360) \times 365 = $197,708.33.$$

Again principal and interest are returned at maturity. For convenience sake, I have used the same interest rate for a deposit payable in dollars or in gold. In the real market the gold rate would have been slightly lower, as per the above.

Where gold is lent for periods longer than one year, the interest is generally paid semiannually, again based on the value of gold at the outset of the trade.

Another way in which gold can be lent is via lease rate swaps, also known as gold interest rate swaps, or just as IRS. This is dealt with in more depth in the next chapter.

6

Bullion Banks

⊰[Major Trading Centers]⊱

 I am no great fan of the phrase "bullion banks," since it seems to be a somewhat ungainly expression, but it is one that simply describes banks involved in the precious metals markets. Traditionally, Asia/Pacific trading operations were based in Sydney to enable the banks to service the gold mining community, and in particular the prolific hedging activities of the Australian producers, with banks perhaps having other trading centers in Hong Kong or Singapore to supply the physical business (small bars). Tokyo was, and still is, obviously the center for the large Japanese trading houses (rather than banks like Sumitomo, Mitsubishi, and Mitsui). Moving on to Europe, London has always been the main center, but it was supported by thriving operations in Zurich, Geneva, and Luxembourg. Once the business crosses the Atlantic, there is only one important center, and that is New York. Once the market there closes, there is no significant interbank and/or market-making presence until the Asian day once again resumes.

However, the rapid consolidation of the Australian mining industry in the late 1990s, which led, in many instances, to the treasury operations being shifted to Johannesburg or the Americas, meant a sorely diminished customer base. The quieter market conditions that were then prevailing saw rationalization in the industry, with most banks only having one trading operation in each time zone and with others sharply curtailing their market-making operations or pulling out of the business completely.

Similarly, it made little sense for an organization to offer market making from London, Geneva, and Zurich, as Credit Suisse used to do before exiting the business almost completely in 2001. London became the uncontested preeminent center for European trading. However, in subdued markets, the question then turned to the cost savings from rationalizing operations between Europe and the Americas. Did it make sense to have two complete trading teams based in London and New York when the time difference was only five hours? Particularly as COMEX (see Chapter 7 on exchanges) shut its doors at 2:30 p.m. and with it closed the trading day. For many banks the solution was simple: London should be the center covering both time zones but working longer hours. Obviously this is now considerably easier with New York/COMEX now closing at 1:30 p.m. local time, thus allowing London traders to leave at 6:30 p.m. their time.

I have lived and worked in all the major gold-trading centers. Each one has different conventions, customers, and sometimes market makers. However, there are also a great number of similarities. Rather than delve into the minutiae of each particular country, I want to look at their similarities. For this I am mainly going to refer to London, not because it is where I am based, but because it straddles Asia and the Americas as well as being the place where gold "clears" (more on that later in this chapter).

The London Bullion Market Association (LBMA) defines the London market as a "wholesale market, where minimum traded amounts for clients are generally 1,000 ounces of gold and 50,000 ounces of silver. It is an OTC (over-the-counter) market, not an exchange."

The LBMA describes itself as "the trade association that acts as the co-ordinator for activities conducted on behalf of its members and other participants in the London bullion market. It acts as the principal point of contact between the market and its regulators. Through its staff and its committees, it works to ensure that London continues to meet the evolving needs of the global bullion market."

·◦[Market Makers]◦·

The market-making members of the London market recognized by the LBMA are:

- The Bank of Nova Scotia–ScotiaMocatta

- Barclays Bank PLC

- Bear Stearns Forex Inc.

- Deutsche Bank AG

- Goldman Sachs International

- HSBC Bank USA NA

- JP Morgan Chase Bank

- Mitsui & Co. Precious Metals Inc., London Branch

- Royal Bank of Canada Limited

- Société Générale

- UBS AG

So just 11 names form the core of the London market; the list still includes Bear Stearns although it would seem doubtful that this will be the case for much longer. This number is something of a surprise to many people, who imagine that the gold market is roughly equivalent to the foreign exchange markets and particularly as it is often mentioned along with the dollar, the euro, the yen, and the sterling as an essential for central bank reserves. A few years ago, when turnover was low, the daily turnover in the gold market was roughly equivalent to that of the Polish zloty or Taiwanese dollar. It is now similar to that of the New Zealand or Canadian dollar. Times have changed, but gold is still a relatively small market.

The Asian and the American time zones have a similar number of interbank market makers but do not have an organization such as the LBMA that codifies this. The other important point about this list is that although the LBMA identifies these 11 institutions as market makers, a host of other institutions are prepared to make markets to their clients, but are price takers (or market users) of those banks listed above.

◦⧾ How Does Spot Gold Trade? ⧽◦

When a bank based in Hong Kong trades with one in London, they trade loco London. This trade has nothing to do with where either bank is based but simply where the metal "clears." So similarly when, for example, Mitsui Busan (Hong Kong) trades with Barclays Bank (Singapore), they too trade loco London. While I go into more details about clearing later, the simplest definition is where accounts settle—so gold trades "loco London" in the same way that U.S. dollars trade "loco New York" and yen trade "loco Tokyo."

The unit of trading is the troy ounce and not the avoirdupois ounce. The latter is the one that we are used to in our daily lives whereas the former is the unit for precious metal trading. The troy ounce is roughly 10 percent larger than the avoirdupois (the exact calculation is that one troy ounce is equivalent to 1.09714 avoirdupois). As mentioned previously, wherever ounces are mentioned in relation to gold in this book, the reference is to troy ounces.

Whereas the LBMA talks of minimum amounts to clients of 1,000 (troy) ounces of gold, the interbank standard quantity is 5,000 or 10,000 ounces. The underlying unit is assumed to be a London Good Delivery bar—defined in full in Chapter 2, but in short a bar weighing between 350 and 430 ounces, which is 0.995 gold (995 parts per thousand and generally spoken of as "two nines five"). In reality the bars generally weigh a few ounces either side of 400, and market shorthand assumes that a bar weighs exactly 400 ounces.

Thus, when one trader makes another a $975/ $976 gold price, then essentially they are saying that at $975 they would be prepared to buy gold conforming to the specification laid down by the LBMA. However, 5,000 is not evenly divisible by 400, and 12.5 bars of gold is a somewhat tricky concept. Neither is it practical to have security trucks loaded with gold whizzing through the streets of London. Hence the gold that is generally traded is "unallocated," so that a price of $975 is the bid for an amount of loco London unallocated gold of 99.5 percent purity, and so on. It is worth noting that it is a fine ounce that is actually traded, so what you buy at $975 is the actual gold content rather than the gross weight.

If you own a quantity of allocated gold, then your statement from the custodian will detail the bar reference number, its purity, and its fine weight. Assuming you were allowed into the vault, then you could see your gold in its own area (often in a separate cage). However, if you own unallocated gold, then your statement would simply detail the amount of ounces in the account. Probably the best analogy is between a checking or current account (unallocated) and a safe deposit box (allocated gold). If you put dollar bills into a safe deposit box, you know their serial numbers and they are segregated, but if you have your money in a checking account, it is part of the general mass.

The exception to this generalization is central banks. Commonly, when central banks trade (spot, forwards, or options), they are trading allocated gold held in their accounts at the Bank of England. Since central banks and members of the LBMA are both allowed to have accounts there, then it is just a simple transfer from one to the other of the various (defined and listed) bars. However, rather than deal 10,000 ounces of gold, for example, the actual quantity needs to be far more exact as it relates to the fine gold content of 25 bars of gold (10,000 divided by 400), so it could be something like 10,006.145 ounces—gold is generally given to three decimal places.

While the normal interbank quantity of gold might be 5,000 or 10,000 ounces, there are a variety of other terms that might be employed by traders and their customers. Rather less common now, outside the gold fixing, is someone trading 5 or 10 bars (4,000 ounces as being 10 bars of 400 ounces each). However, it is not uncommon to trade a tonne; this is assumed to be 32,000 ounces, which is rather different from the precise calculation of a metric tonne of 32,150.70 troy ounces. Equally a trader might be asked for markets in half a tonne, and so forth.

So generally the terminology swings seamlessly between a medieval weight, bars, and metric tonnes (of 1,000 kilograms). However, the market also is equally comfortable using the traditional Indian measurement of lakh, meaning 100,000. Thus being asked for "gold in a lakh" would mean someone requesting a price in 100,000 ounces, similarly a half and quarter of a lakh. While the formal spelling is "lakh," on the market it is generally written as "lac."

Thus, depending on circumstances, a trader might be asked for a price in ounces, bars, tonnes, or lacs. This may sound unwieldy, but it is quickly picked up and widely adopted. Indeed, for the silver market, it is virtually inconceivable that someone might ask a price in "two hundred thousand ounces," but a very common request for silver in "two lacs."

To clarify a point made previously, I note that in OTC markets the price is for an ounce of fine gold. Theoretically, if you pay $975 for an ounce of gold, it will then physically weigh more than an ounce to account for the impurities. Another way of looking at it is if you were to buy a bar of gold of 401.213 gross weight and a fineness of 0.9957, then you would actually be getting 399.488 ounces of gold, and the cost would be this amount multiplied by the spot rate.

⋅∘[Liquidity]∘⋅

Given that there are 11 spot market makers in London, the greatest concentration globally, then effectively any price request for a quantity over 50,000 ounces of gold becomes significant, the trader offsetting his risk by trading with the other 10 institutions. Realistically though, in the current erratic trading environment almost any quantity can become unwieldy with prices moving rapidly. However, customers can obtain markets in much greater sizes than this with the overall liquidity, and hence the interbank traders' exit strategy, enhanced by exchanges and niche market makers who will only quote their client base or show a bid or offer through the brokers.

The method a trader uses to offset risk will vary, based on the quantity that has been traded and the market environment. Traditionally, the only tool available to a London-based market maker was to sell to other traders, as it is an OTC market. Whereas in New York a dealer would probably hedge most of the risk by trading COMEX/NYMEX and in Asia it would be a combination of one of the local exchanges (Tokyo Commodity Exchange, or TOCOM, is the largest) and direct OTC trades with other market makers.

More recently, the advent of global screen-based exchanges that operate more or less on a 24-hour basis has blurred such precise distinctions, so that traders will all use a combination of OTC and exchanges to manage risk—the working of various exchanges are covered in Chapter 7.

Having just outlined these methods, it is difficult to generalize, although I am going to do just that and say that if someone is looking to trade a "significant quantity"—over a ton, i.e., more than 32,000 ounces—then the simplest and/or quickest way to conduct this transaction is going to be in the OTC market.

In some instances though, institutions need to trade at a "benchmark," a published price that is a matter of record. For the gold market this is invariably the London Gold Fixing.

⁓⦊ The London Gold Fixing ⦉⁓

Given that the first gold fixing took place in 1919, I could use this as an opportunity to embark on a historical tangent on its workings. However, as I stated in the introduction, this book is not intended as a record of previous practices except where they affect the current operation of the market. For those who would like to see the timeline, I would recommend the Web site of www.goldfixing.com. The longest fixing took place on March 23, 1990—caused by a Middle East institution selling a large quantity of gold and buying sterling with it—the price dropping over $20 during the course of this 2-hour, 26-minute marathon, but more typically a fixing is over in 5 to 10 minutes.

That aside, the gold fixing takes place twice daily, at 10:30 a.m. and 3:00 p.m. London time—not GMT as is sometimes reported. The members are:

- The Bank of Nova Scotia–ScotiaMocatta

- Barclays Bank PLC

- Deutsche Bank AG

- HSBC Bank USA NA

- Société Générale

While the names have changed over the years, there have always been five members, and all of these own an equal share in the company that administers the fixing, The London Gold Market Fixing Ltd.

In previous years, representatives met at the London offices of N.M. Rothschild who traditionally chaired the fixing. This might have worked extremely well for many of the last 90 years but as the financial district of London expanded it became considerably less convenient with some organizations having to send staff on a 15-minute train ride twice a day to get them from Canary Wharf to Rothschild's headquarters near the Bank of England.

Indeed there were a number of discussions about moving to either a computer- or phone-based system. Progress had been somewhat slow, but when Rothschild exited the gold market in 2004—citing the declining percentage of total income that commodity trading contributed to their overall profits—the decision was taken to end the tradition of the fixing being held in a specific location. Instead, it was conducted over the phone.

Barclays Bank was the newcomer to the fixing at this time, buying the seat vacated by Rothschild. This change also saw the chairing of the fixing rotate on an annual basis. Although the mechanism might have been updated a little, the terminology and methodology remain unchanged.

The fixing now takes place over a dedicated conference line, with each of the five members represented. It starts with the chair suggesting an initial price. This price is then communicated to the five trading rooms, which in turn inform clients via phone, Reuters dealer, Bloomberg instant messaging, Yahoo, and so on; in many instances, these secondary organizations will then inform their clients. At each price any client can buy, sell, or do nothing. All of this information is then collated in the dealing rooms of the five members until it is just a simple amount that needs to be bought, or sold, or is netted off to zero.

Thus each member declares his or her interest over the phone as buyer, seller, or "no interest." If there are buyers and sellers, or if there are just two of either of those (plus three "no interest"), then the chair will "call for figures," also known as "trying figures." Each of the five members gives their requested amount in multiples of five bars (of a notional 400 ounces each—metal at the fixing is unallocated). If there is a difference of 50 bars or less between the buyers and sellers, then the price is "fixed"—or indeed between the buyers or sellers and the "no interests," with the outstanding balance being divided among the members. Similarly, gold can also be called "fixed" if each of the five banks declares itself a "no interest"—the conclusion being that the market is in equilibrium at that time.

Traditionally, the selling figures were declared first, perhaps owing in part to one of the original purposes of the fixing to assist the nascent South African mining industry. While this nicety has largely disappeared, the convention is observed in that market shorthand always gives the selling figure first, be it the number of sellers or the bars themselves. Thus "three and one" would mean that there are three sellers and one buyer, whereas "80 against 20" would mean that 80 bars were offered but only 20 were wanted.

If indeed the balance in the room were 80/20, with everyone having declared their interest, the next price to try would be lower, in an attempt to attract buyers and to dissuade sellers. Clearly the situation would be the reverse if the figure were 20/80.

In another piece of relevant history, if a bank were to wish to change the quantity that they have declared or indeed to change their position—from buyer to seller, or the like—then they are said to "flag." This term may sound somewhat bizarre, but the phrase was historically very accurate, although the nature of the act was somewhat odd. When the fixings were held at N.M. Rothschild, each of the five desks in the room had a small Union Jack on it, all lying on their sides. If a member should wish to alter a declaration, then that member would set the flag upright and call "flag." Gold could not, and cannot, be fixed while "flags are up" or "flags are in the room." The same terminology is used in the same way currently, although the Union Jack is now purely figurative.

The attraction of the fixing as a benchmark is clear, since it denotes a market that is clearly in balance at that time. Transaction costs are generally very reasonable as well, with both buyers and sellers transacting at a premium over the fixing price. This premium might be 5 cents over for sellers and 25 cents charged to buyers. In some instances, it might not be 05/25 but 10/20, in market parlance. The five members transact "in the room" (metaphorical as it might be) in the middle at 15 cents.

·◌] Trading Gold Interest Rates [◌·

In Chapter 5, I detail the borrowers and lenders. In this chapter I want to examine more closely how this market is actually traded.

At its simplest the trading would just be a series of deposits and loans taking place. A central bank lends gold to Barclays, which lends it to a gold producer, which hedges gold that it has yet to produce, and so on. However, trades are not just washed through in exact amounts and tenors (transcripts) from one institution to another. No currency market would operate in such a fashion; nor would a series of deposits and/or loans make any sense, since the exposure between institutions would build up rapidly and become unwieldy.

Instead, central banks tend to lend gold as a deposit—so full principal risk for the central bank lies on the bullion bank. The banks then trade between themselves via a series of instruments that are designed to mitigate that credit exposure simply to prevent credit lines from being tied up—given the likely high volume of transactions across all traded products. For short-dated trades, the most common mechanism is a gold swap, also known as a gold forward. In base metals it would be known as a carry trade and in money markets as a repo (sale and repurchase agreement).

Although this is a gold-lending transaction, the mechanism by which it is achieved is via a sale and subsequent repurchase of the metal. The difference in the two prices is calculated using the swap rate, which itself is the theoretical net of U.S. dollar and gold interest rates.

An example should make this clearer: Bank A asks Bank B for a six-month gold swap. The price of 2.35/2.45 percent is made. What this means is that at 2.35 percent Bank B would be prepared to lend gold (via a sale and repurchase) and at 2.45 percent they would be prepared to borrow gold (via a purchase and then a sale). Despite the use of "buy" and "sell," these types of transactions have absolutely no impact on the spot price for gold.

Assuming that Bank A is a borrower of 100,000 ounces and trades at 2.35 percent:

On Day 1, Bank B sells 100,000 ounces of gold at $975.00 to Bank A.

On Day 180, Bank B buys 100,000 ounces of gold at $986.456 from Bank A.

The forward price is calculated as:

$$\$975 + (((\$975 \times 2.35\%)/360) \times 180)$$
$$= \$975 + \$11.456 = \$986.456$$

Gold price + (((gold price × gold swap rate)/360) × day count)

On the face of it, Bank B has booked a loss on the trade:

$$100,000 \times \$11.456 = \$1,145,600$$

However, from the initial transaction, Bank B has generated $97.5 million (100,000 ounces of gold sold at $975 per ounce), which it places on deposit for six months at a rate of 2.50 percent, and this generates interest of $1,218,750.

So Bank B's net profit on the transaction is $73,150 (the interest profit of $1,218,750 less the capital loss of $1,145,600), assuming that they paid zero for the gold originally—which is unlikely, but I just wanted to demonstrate the concept.

Another way of looking at the profit is that it is the net of 2.35 percent (where Bank B borrowed the dollars and lent the gold) and 2.50 percent (where it managed to place the dollars on deposit). This amount of 15-basis points (0.15 percent) is the return for lending gold for six months in this example.

Thus the gold swap rate is the net of U.S. dollar and gold interest rates. It is the gold swap rate market that is the main instrument for short-dated gold trading, and it is this that ultimately drives the lease/deposit market.

Incidentally, the rationale for a central bank lending via a deposit (full principal risk) and a commercial bank via swaps (mitigated risk) is not quite as bizarre as it might sound. First, the sheer volume of trades between two market-making institutions is likely to be enormous, so rather than have a jumble of outstandings that might or might not net off, it is a lot easier to mitigate credit risk at the outset. Secondly, if a central bank were to lend via swaps, then it would generate dollars that would have to be lent to a bank, thus generating the credit risk it tried to avoid in the first place! However, some central banks have used their gold reserves as a form of financing tool—the gold is effectively collateral in a loan.

Interestingly enough, during the recent credit crunch, a two-tier market developed for gold deposits from central banks. Although the highly rated banks might be paying 20 basis points for a 12-month gold deposit from a central bank, I have heard of instances where lenders were being bid 45 basis points by some less credit-worthy bullion banks. The attractiveness for the borrower, even paying wildly above the market, was that this gold could subsequently be swapped in the interbank market, thus generating relatively cheap cash for the institution that might be experiencing liquidity constraints.

For longer-dated transactions the normal style of market transaction is a lease rate swap, gold interest rate swap (or just an IRS, as it is now more commonly referred to). Similarly to the money market instrument—from which it is derived—in market parlance the borrower would pay fixed and receive floating. Or in other words, they would borrow fixed-term gold and lend back short-dated. Crucially the gold does not change hands, so it is less credit intensive, but instead it is the underlying cash flows that are paid and/or received. An example follows:

Bank C asks Bank D for a 10-year IRS. A price of 0.65/0.75 percent is quoted. What this means is that at 0.65 percent Bank D would be prepared to borrow 10-year gold (and lend it back quarterly), and at the other side of the spread Bank D would be lending the long-dated gold and borrowing it back quarterly.

Assuming that Bank C is a lender of the long-dated gold, then it would trade this at 0.65 percent, lending 10-year gold at that rate and borrowing back over a series of three months. Conversely Bank D borrows 100,000 at 0.65 percent for 10 years and lends 40 periods of three months each.

Day 1: Bank D agrees that in three months time it will pay Bank C:

$$(((\text{Amount of gold} \times \text{fixed interest rate})/360) \times \text{day count})$$

$$(((100,000 \times 0.65\%)/360) \times 90) = 162.50 \text{ ounces of gold.}$$

Bank C agrees that in three months time it will pay Bank D:

$$((\text{Amount of gold} \times \text{floating interest rate}))/360$$
$$\times \text{day count}((100,000 \times 0.16857\%))/360$$
$$\times 90 = 42.143 \text{ ounces of gold.}$$

Thus net Bank D will pay Bank C 120.357 (i.e., $162 - 42.143$) ounces of gold.

To get the floating interest rate requires a benchmark rate. There is no such number for gold interest rates in the way that there is for currencies. Therefore, convention is that the number is derived from LIBOR minus GOFO (which is exactly how the market refers to it). LIBOR refers to the benchmark rate for U.S. dollar interest lending rates (published on Reuters page LIBOR) and the benchmark for gold swap/forward rates—GOld FOrward reduced to GOFO, which is also the page where it appears on the Reuters data services.

On the day when I was writing this:

The three-month U.S. dollar LIBOR was 2.71 percent.

The three-month GOFO was 2.54143 percent.

Thus net (LIBOR − GOFO) was 0.16857 percent.

The GOFO benchmark is calculated on a daily basis at 11 a.m. London time. It accepts contributions from nine banks, the highest and lowest swap rates are discounted, and the final figure is derived from the arithmetic mean of the other seven institutions.

The rationale behind trading IRS is that it is both a credit-effective way of transacting long-term gold interest rates as well as looking to take advantage of changes in the shape of the curve—i.e., if short-term interest rates start to spike and move above the fixed rate (in the case of an institution that is paying fixed and receiving floating interest amounts).

When central banks lend gold for the long term—realistically in excess of 2 years—they are generally unwilling to take commercial bank credit for periods that might be as long as 10 years. Therefore, to mitigate this risk they either lend gold on a collateralized basis (the borrowers have to place government bonds with the lender to the same value as the gold, which is reassessed weekly or monthly), or they could enter into an IRS. The problem for the central banks, though, is that a standard IRS does not involve the movement of gold, and the motive for the central banks is to earn a yield on their gold. They do this by lending long-term gold via an IRS, borrowing back the (three-month) gold under the terms of an IRS, but then separately lending gold for the (three-month) short-dated period as well. This may all sound unnecessarily complicated, but in essence it means that they effectively receive a 10-year rate for their gold lending by entering into a series of short-dated trades (40 × 3 months).

⌐[The Gold Option Market]⌐

The gold option market functions in much the same way as any currency market. Indeed gold is often thought of as a currency, although there is admittedly some debate as to whether it is actually a currency or simply a commodity. The safest reply is probably that it has characteristics of both.

The rapid growth in the gold option market (particularly during the 1990s) was driven by the gold mining companies. It occurred for three reasons. First, many of them were consistent sellers of gold call options; second, they were a dominant force for price movements; and third, many of the hedging transactions were large in size and complex.

The rationale for many miners when selling gold call options was twofold. Not only did they recognize that gold was in a long-term bear market, but the premium earned from selling these options was also a welcome addition to working capital. In most instances the tenor was no more than six months, and some were extremely active in selling options with low delta (small probability of being exercised) for no more than one month, almost seen as money for nothing in the then prevailing bearish environment. However, this complacency meant that there had been rumors that some small mining companies ended up by selling more call options than their total production for some periods. Indeed this was rumored to be behind some of the difficulties faced by certain mining companies when gold spiked following the central bank gold agreement in September 1999: The price of the options suddenly became too expensive to buy back, and they had insufficient gold production to meet the calls that were being exercised.

The producers were as dominant in call selling as they were in put buying—obviously their natural hedge—so that a major skew arose in put volatility, and it was much more expensive than that for calls.

To generalize, not particularly unfairly, during the hedging heyday of the market, the independent Australian producers were the most active. They were also extremely innovative—or at least very interested in entering into innovative trades—and prepared to use linkages across markets and structures that defaulted into different basis risk. Indeed, when I was part of a presentation team to a mining company in the late 1990s, they were not interested in any of the more vanilla structures but wanted the most leveraged option possible; they were sellers and wanted to realize the greatest amount of premium.

The trouble was that there was little in the way of effectively measuring the risk for many of these institutions and in certain instances they did not, or could not, stress-test their books to see what would happen under various scenarios. Again the result was considerable angst when the gold market started to rally, first during late 1999 and then in subsequent years. I remember helping an Australian company evaluate their hedges, which had a high degree of linkage between spot gold and gold interest rates. For example, should gold rise, this would then ratchet up the interest rate they needed to pay for borrowing gold. Thus a sudden rapid spike in prices would have led to an untenable and unmanageable situation for the miner. Hence they subsequently restructured their book to help protect against this eventuality.

They were not alone in this type of hedgebook activity; in most instances these positions were unwound and the small independent producers were taken over by large offshore companies.

The demands of the gold producers at this time saw a period of great innovation in the type of option structures that could be entered into. First of all there were just vanilla puts and calls; these were soon joined by barrier options, window and anniversary barriers, digitals, quantos, and so on. Most of these were designed to meet the pay-off requirements of the mining industry, although many of the ideas were imported from the foreign exchange and fixed income markets.

Obviously matters are very different now. The producers are far less inclined to hedge; indeed, that business has almost entirely ground to a halt. Pronouncements by miners on this topic are far more likely to be that they have foresworn this activity—and the only exception really is when banks demand hedging as a precondition of lending money to a new project—in effect prudent cash-flow protection.

·≈| Hedge Funds |≈·

Hedge funds have been active in the gold market for many years. However, the rapidly growing amount of assets under management (AUM)—now estimated to be $1.875 trillion—has seen their influence increase rapidly even as that of the producers has declined. Indeed, for the 1990s it was undoubtedly the gold mining companies and the central banks (to fund the hedges) that were the most actively targeted customers for bullion banks; now, unquestionably, it is hedge funds.

Initially, hedge fund activity in gold was limited to specialist commodity funds with considerable input from macro funds with longstanding commodity interest. For those who are unaware of what a "macro hedge fund" actually is, basically they do not specialize in any one particular market or sector, instead their expertise and product suite is wide ranging. However, the rapid growth in AUM has meant that funds are increasingly looking to new markets in which to invest. The fact that this rapid increase in the power of this particular sector has coincided with the decline in U.S. dollar was a considerable help to the gold price.

While there are people who are interested in gold, be they "gold bugs" or just enthusiasts for its own purposes, for many it had become an obsolete form of investment. Why bother to invest in gold as an inflation hedge when you can buy Treasury Inflation-Protected Securities (TIPS) instead? People fleeing oppression and war do not need gold; all they need is a halfway decent banking system, or Internet connection, to transfer money overseas. Central banks had never enjoyed such high levels of esteem or belief in their powers to rein in inflation. Gold generally has no yield for the small, private, investor, so what was the point of investing in it? Indeed, being in the gold market during the dot-com boom looked to be a lesson in futility.

This trend was the ultimate expression of how gold had been marginalized. Entrepreneurs were creating enormous wealth with little more than a business plan, what did people need with a stale and stagnant gold market? Clearly there were much better places for investment; indeed for many the ideal trade would have been to short gold (the ultimate expression of the "old economy") while buying technology stocks.

The change in the fortunes of many Internet stocks and the U.S. dollar has been a wake-up call for the attractions of gold; hence the belief of hedge funds in this market that has seen them become a significant influence. Once more they are looking at products similar to those that they use in other markets to participate in the rise of gold. However, no one should be under any illusions; this interest is rarely long term. It is not a replacement for buying from central banks; instead it is taking advantage of the current market outlook. Once this view changes, there will be no emotional attachment to gold. Instead there is the possibility of finding a very crowded exit.

In many situations, hedge funds will go with the consensus view (or perhaps create it). They certainly have little interest in being continual sellers of call options in rising or falling markets. Instead they will tend to buy call options if they believe the market is rising (or sell puts) and the converse in falling markets. Hence, in rising markets, there is a premium for call volatility over that for puts and the opposite when prices are falling.

For the interbank option market there are probably just six "first division" players with another four on the second tier. The standard interbank quote is 50 to 100,000 ounces (half a lac or a lac) out to one year but volumes tend to fall away after that. Large customers can fairly easily obtain prices in considerably larger volume. The standard convention within the gold market has been to ask for a gold call or put, perhaps even as "an Aussie gold call." However, the market is increasingly adopting language garnered from the foreign exchange market such that it is commonly referred to as a gold call U.S. dollar put or perhaps a gold put Aussie dollar call, and so on.

Generally though, market makers will tend to make markets in gold against the U.S. dollar, Australian dollars, euros, and the South African rand—Aussie dollars and the rand being holdovers from the days of hedging from the mining industry. Realistically though, the U.S.-dollar gold option market accounts for some 80 percent of all business, the Australian dollar a further 10 percent, and the other currencies are very much also-rans.

While, theoretically, it is no harder to make prices against the Canadian dollar, Swiss franc, or Japanese yen, the vol (market shorthand for volatility) bid offer spread will tend to be considerably wider and only really entered into for significant business.

In the end, all business, be it spot, forward, or options, needs to be "cleared."

⊰ Clearing ⊱

As mentioned previously, London is the clearing center for gold in exactly the same way that the U.S. dollar clears through New York and the yen through Tokyo. The London Bullion Market Association (LBMA) defines this process as follows: "The London bullion market relies on a daily clearing system of paper transfers. Members offering clearing services utilise the unallocated gold and silver accounts they maintain between each other for the settlement of mutual trades as well as third party transfers. These transfers are conducted on behalf of clients and other members of the London bullion market in settlement of their own loco London bullion activities. This system avoids the security risks and costs that would be involved in the physical movement of bullion."

Indeed the notion of a succession of trucks laden with gold bullion making their way through the streets of the City of London, and its environs, would create a logistical and security nightmare, as well as significantly increase transaction costs. Anecdotally, a couple of short examples illustrate this scenario. One story is that of a European central bank that had entered into a gold-lending program, all of which with the same maturity date. Because the gold had to be returned to the Bank of England, a line of armored trucks was parked outside that institution's vaults while the metal was unloaded. Suffice it to say, that particular trading strategy was never used again. Another story involves an armored truck managing to hit the security doors of a clearer's vaults, rendering the depository out of action for several days. Clearly accidents do happen and it is sensible to avoid them wherever possible.

There are six companies that offer a clearing service and they are joint owners of a company called London Precious Metals Clearing Limited (LPMCL). The members are:

- Barclays Bank PLC

- The Bank of Nova Scotia–ScotiaMocatta

- Deutsche Bank AG–London Branch

- HSBC Bank USA National Association–London Branch

- JP Morgan Chase Bank

- UBS AG

Traditionally, banks tended to provide clearing services free of charge because vaults were unlikely to ever be full of metal, which meant that the clearers could lend out balances held in their vaults (unallocated only), which in turn mitigated the cost. This service worked very well when there was a vibrant lending/borrowing market. However, when turnover sharply decreased (the virtual demise of the gold hedging market is covered in Chapter 4), vaults did start to fill and there was little call to borrow gold.

It was at this time that a once free service began to be charged for; indeed one-month interest rates were trading at −10 basis points (minus 0.1 percent) at one point, and thus storage of gold just became a charge with no possibility of lending the metal to cover costs.

While the metal can theoretically be transferred throughout the trading day, in practice it tends to happen just prior to 4 p.m., London time, when transfers should stop, except by mutual consent.

There is one extremely important institution that also clears metal but has not been mentioned above and is not a part owner of LPMCL; it is the Bank of England. The vaults of the bank lie outside the clearing system because all movements there are allocated, hence the above-described truck lineup. In other words specific bars are transferred from one account to another. The largest group of institutions that choose to maintain their accounts at the Bank of England are the central banks; by contrast, I can think of only six countries that maintain unallocated accounts at a clearer (and most of these have accounts at the Bank of England as well).

·∘⟦ Turnover ⟧∘·

In the London market—where gold of course clears for OTC transactions—the relevant data are compiled by the LBMA, which collates, on a monthly basis, information provided to it from the six members offering clearing services (LPMCL). Three measures are taken separately for each metal:

   ⟦∘ *Volume*: the amount of metal transferred on average each day measured in millions of troy ounces. (See Figure 6–1.)

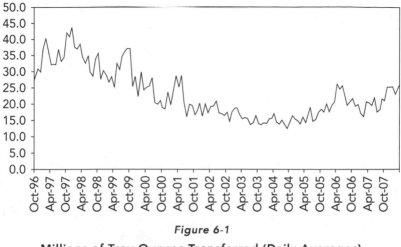

Figure 6-1

Millions of Troy Ounces Transferred (Daily Averages)

Source: LBMA

> *Value*: the value measured in U.S. dollars, using the monthly average London p.m. fixing price for gold. (See Figure 6–2.)

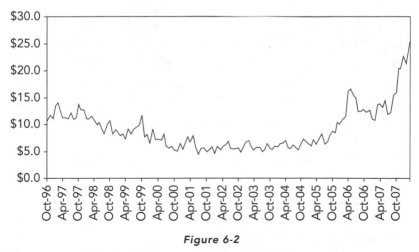

Figure 6-2

Value in Billions of Dollars (Daily Average)

Source: LBMA

ǀ⊙ *Number of Transfers*: the average number recorded each day. (See Figure 6–3.)

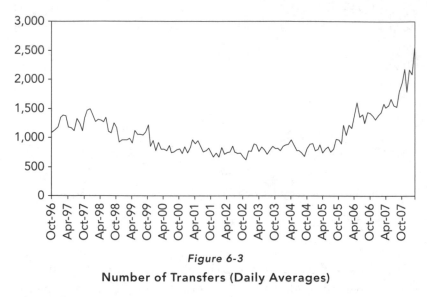

Figure 6-3
Number of Transfers (Daily Averages)

Source: LBMA

It is worth remembering that gold is a small market with OTC/ loco London settlement of normally less than $15 billion on a daily basis, although currently running at its highest ever level of $25 billion (but not in terms of number of ounces or number of transfers, in part due to lower activity in the lending market). Admittedly turnover is likely to be a multiple of settled ounces, particularly adding in the various exchanges. It is difficult to put any sort of exact number on it, but taking an educated guess it would seem sensible to equate the gold market with being somewhere between the USDCAD (U.S. dollar versus Canadian dollar) and USDCHF (U.S. dollar versus Swiss franc) markets. Incidentally, the global foreign exchange market turns over some $3 trillion on a daily basis.

⸙[Market Conventions]⸙

Spot Market Making. The general interbank "clip" is for 5,000 to 10,000 ounces of gold. However, it is standard for all price requests to include the quantity. Thus market shorthand is "gold in 10k" or similarly expressed. Market makers do not ask each other in prices for smaller than 5,000 ounces as it is assumed, rightly, that they are risk takers with a flow of transactions through their books and lesser quantities would be unprofessional.

Aside from the 11 London market makers listed earlier in this chapter, a number of institutions are prepared to provide prices to their customer base but not to other market makers. These market users will either try and "broker" transactions to the market makers making a small turn on the trade or will hedge their risk through the myriad exchanges (which are covered in Chapter 7).

Options Market Making. The standard quantity is 50,000 to 100,000 ounces, but it will depend on tenor, volatility, delta, and currency pairing. In regard to customers, the same comments apply here as above.

Forwards Market Making. Once again, the standard traded quantity is 50,000 to 100,000 ounces but will be very much dependent on tenor, with customers often able to gather quotes in increased size at more favorable terms.

Gold Exchanges

 Throughout this book, it has been my intention to approach and thus start with the various exchanges in Asia before proceeding to the United States via the newest player in Dubai, as well as the ever-present online futures markets. My apologies if I have omitted a particular institution, but I have concentrated on those markets where professionals tend to focus their attention.

·◦⟨ TOCOM (Japan) ⟩◦·

TOCOM is the universally adopted acronym for the Tokyo Commodity Exchange. It defines itself (www.tocom.or.jp) as follows: "TOCOM is a non-profit membership organization as defined under the Commodity Exchange Act (1950), which regulates all commodities futures and options trading in Japan."

The specifications of the contract that is traded there, again from the exchange's Web site, are listed as follows:

Date of Listing: March 23, 1982
Type of Trade: Physical Delivery Futures Transaction
Standard: Fine gold of minimum 99.99 percent purity
Trading Method: Computerized continuous trading

Contract Months: All even months within a year (on the day when a new contract month is generated, there will be six even months starting from the next even month after the month which the said day belongs to)

Last Trading Day: The third business day prior to the Delivery Day

Delivery Day: The last day of each even month except December (the 24th for December). If the day is a holiday or a half-day holiday, Delivery Day is advanced.

Delivery Points: Specified warehouses

Trading Hours: 9:00 a.m. to 11:00 a.m., 12:30 p.m. to 5:30 p.m.

Contract Unit: 1 kilogram/contract

Delivery Unit: 1 kilogram/contract

Price Quotation: Japanese yen per gram

Minimum Price Fluctuation: One Japanese yen per gram

Daily Price Fluctuation Limit: Daily price fluctuation limits are determined based on the largest market price movement within a certain time period and set at a level where the probability that they will be reached is very low.

In addition to the underlying contract, you need to know how to actually trade on the exchange. Here too the TOCOM Web site sets out its order and/or execution system.

The following describes the methods for participating in TOCOM's markets from overseas:

1. As a member, to access TOCOM's markets directly, you are required to obtain Market Membership and install a TOCOM trading terminal in Japan (direct access).

2. Members without a trading terminal can trade on TOCOM's markets through TOCOM Broker Members (Indirect access—through Futures Commission Merchants or FCMs).

3. In either case, eligibility for membership is limited to foreign FCMs and persons or firms engaged in the

purchase or sale, brokerage, production, processing or use of commodities listed on the Exchange, who meet certain financial and other qualifications. In addition, certain financial obligations are required to be a member.

4. As an Associate Member: Overseas traders who deal with commodities listed on TOCOM's markets and belong to certain organizations specified by TOCOM are eligible for Associate Membership. Associate Membership is like a special favoured customer status, that is, Associate Members must place orders through Broker Members and have no right of voting at general meetings, but the same margin rates as Members' are applied to Associate Members.

5. As a customer: You can place an order as a customer with a Broker Member. Also, your order can be accepted by a Foreign FCM who places the order through a Broker Member to TOCOM.

All of the above is useful information, but for the majority of us, we simply need to know how it relates to the loco London gold price and if there is an effective arbitrage.

Because TOCOM gold contracts are only available for alternate even-numbered months, the eleventh or twelfth month forward is the active contract, depending on the actual date (i.e., in January it is December that is the most traded, and in July it is June, and so on. So to determine whether there is an effective arbitrage, we need to convert yen per gram for delivery in 11 months, for example, to U.S. dollars per troy ounce for delivery in two days. Added to which there is a difference in the underlying bar size (kilo rather than 400 ounce) and purity (9999 rather than 995). Finally, there is the difference in delivery location—Tokyo against London.

The final conundrum is that foreign traders have occasionally been uncertain as to their rights to deliver onto the exchange. The rules seem to be somewhat clearer for Japanese houses based there, in which case the arbitrage can "blow out" rather farther than the pure mathematics would suggest. Consequently, most foreign institutions choose not to deliver metal into TOCOM.

The rough calculation itself is as follows:

L = Loco London spot price in dollars per ounce.

T = TOCOM price expressed in Japanese yen per gram.

C = 32.148 = conversion factor for 9999 purity gold in grams to ounces.

F = Forward foreign exchange rate to convert the contract to U.S. dollars.

S = Swap rate to convert a forward gold price to a spot equivalent.

$$L = [G \times (1,000/32.148)]/\{F \times (1 + S)\}$$

Clearly this is much less complicated once the appropriate spreadsheet has been completed.

The Chinese Gold and Silver Exchange Society (Hong Kong)

Arguably the world's oldest exchange for trading precious metals, it began in 1910 as "Gold and Silver Exchange Company" before changing its name in 1918 to "The Chinese Gold and Silver Exchange Society"—the name it still goes by.

Despite its age, this exchange has lost a considerable amount of its importance from its heyday, which was probably in the 1970s and early 1980s, before it found its position eroded by TOCOM. Once again the units, purity, bar size, location, and so on, all vary from the recognizable spot price for gold.

The exchange currently trades in two methods; one is the "open outcry" method in its trading hall, and the other is the "electronic trading" method via its electronic trading platform, which launched in March of 2008.

Open Outcry Market

The exchange itself varies from TOCOM in that it is an open outcry market and conducted in Cantonese, the local language. Unusually, for any exchange, it has two gold products that are traded. The first is the traditional taels with a kilogram price having been added in 2002. The Web site of the Chinese Gold and Silver Exchange Society (www.cgse.com.hk) defines the contracts as:

Fineness: 99
Trading Lot: 100 taels
Price Indication: Hong Kong dollar per tael
Minimum Price Fluctuation: 0.50 Hong Kong dollar per tael
Premium Calculation: Hong Kong dollar per 100 taels
Premium Fixing: Monday to Friday 11:00 a.m.
Settlement Price: Monday to Friday 11:30 a.m. to 4:30 p.m.
Fineness: 999.9
Trading Lot: 5 kilograms
Price Indication: Hong Kong dollar per gram
Minimum Price Fluctuation: 0.10 Hong Kong dollar per gram
Premium Calculation: Hong Kong dollar per 5 kilograms
Premium Fixing: Monday to Friday 11:15 a.m.
Settlement Price: Monday to Friday 11:30 a.m. to 4:30 p.m.

I doubt whether many people who have not spent time in Asia are particularly conversant with the term *tael*, but it is an ancient Chinese unit of weight, a little larger than a troy ounce. To convert a tael to a troy ounce, the tael amount needs to be divided by 0.831.

Obviously there are again the same issues of purity, bar, location, and so on. However, a very rough guide to convert the price on this Hong Kong exchange to a loco London spot equivalent is:

L = Loco London spot price in dollars per ounce
HK = CGSE Price expressed in HK dollars per tael
C = 1.1913 = conversion factor for 99 purity gold in taels to ounces
F = Foreign exchange rate to convert the contract to U.S. dollars (called the TT rate)
L = HK/1.1913/F

Incidentally, although I spent six years working in Hong Kong's gold markets, I never calculated a price in taels per Hong Kong dollar. I had a physical trader who used the market to arbitrage his positions in the local and/or international markets, as well as helping me manage my loco London positions via the exchange on occasions where there was sufficient liquidity. Instead, whether I was trading with another bank in Hong Kong or with a bank in Tokyo, Sydney, Singapore, Beijing, and so on, we were trading loco London gold between us: in other words, U.S. dollars per troy ounce for settlement in London two days later.

I have not included the calculation for the kilogram contract, as I understand that the turnover has been extremely small.

Electronic Trading Platform

There are two types of contract, which are the 100 oz. Loco London Contract and the 10oz Loco London Contract traded via the electronic system, the details of which are shown below:

Fineness: Pure gold

Trading Lot: 100 ounces and 10 ounces

Price Indication: U.S. dollar per ounce

Minimum Price Fluctuation: U.S. dollar 0.01 per ounce

Settlement Price: Average price at a specific time frame

Premium Calculation: Determined by the Executive and Supervisory Committee, based on a specific time frame

Premium Fixing: With reference from LBMA

Delivery: 400-ounce gold bar of 995 fineness, produced by refinements of the LBMA good delivery list

Trading Hours: (Hong Kong Time) 08:00 a.m. to 03:30 p.m. (next day), Monday through Friday

◦⌐ Shanghai Futures Exchange (China) ⌐◦

On its Web site (http://www.shfe.com.cn/Ehome/index.jsp) the exchange describes itself as "a self-regulated non-profit organization, providing the place, facilities and services for the centralized trading of futures contracts. At present, there are six contracts including copper, aluminum, natural rubber, fuel oil, zinc, and gold futures."

The contract itself is defined on the Shanghai Futures Exchange Web site as:

Underlined Product: Gold

Trading Unit: 1 kilogram/lot

Quotation Unit: yuan (RMB)/gram

Tick Size: 0.01 yuan/gram

Daily Price Limit: Within range of 5 percent above or below the settlement price of the previous trading day

Contract Months: January to December

Trading Hours: 9:00 a.m. to 11:30 a.m., 1:30 p.m. to 3:00 p.m.

Last Trading Day: The 15th day of the spot month (postponed if legal holidays)

Delivery Duration: 16th to 20th day of the spot month (postponed if legal holidays)

Deliverable Grades Domestic Product: Gold with fineness not less than 99.95 percent

Overseas Product: Gold that is regarded by LBMA as good delivery

Delivery Sites: Warehouses designated by the Exchange

Minimum Transaction Margin: 7 percent of contract value

Transaction Fee: Equal to or below 0.02 percent of transaction value (risk reserve included)

Delivery Method: Physical delivery

Symbol: AU

Listed Bourse: SHFE

The six-month forward month is generally the active contract. The approximate calculation to compare this to loco London spot gold is:

L = Loco London spot price in dollars per ounce.

G = SHFE Price expressed in Chinese yuan per gram.

C = 32.1355 conversion factor for 9995 purity gold in grams to ounces.

F = Forward foreign exchange rate to convert the contract to U.S. dollars.

S = Swap rate to convert a forward gold price to a spot equivalent.

$$L = [G \times (1{,}000/32.135)]/\{F \times (1 + S)\}$$

⊰ Dubai Gold and Commodities Exchange (Dubai) ⊱

The Dubai Gold and Commodities Exchange (DGCX) is the newcomer to the stable of gold exchanges and is making a strong push to grow its business. DGCX commenced trading in November 1995 and offers "a fully automated, state-of-the-art, electronic trading platform accessible from anywhere in the world."

On its Web site (www.dgcx.ae), DGCX defines its contract as:

Contract Size: 32 troy ounces (1 kilogram)

Quality Specification: 0.995 purity, as per Dubai good delivery standard

Trading Months: February, April, June, August, October, and December

Last Trading Day: Business day immediately preceding sixth delivery day

New Contract Listing: On the last delivery day

Price Quote: U.S. dollar per troy ounce

Minimum Tick Size: U.S. dollar 0.10

Price Movement Limit: Thirty U.S. dollars (for more details see the Web site)

Maximum Open Position Limit: As determined and specified by the Exchange

Maximum Order Size: 200 contracts

Trading Days: Opening: Monday through Friday

Trading Hours: Monday through Friday, 08:30 a.m. to 11:30 p.m. (GMT + 4)

For delivery:

Delivery Unit: 1 kilogram (31.99 troy ounces)

Deliverable Weight: 1 kilogram cast in one bar

Deliverable Quality: 0.995 fineness

Approved CMI/Assayers: Names as listed on the DGCX Web site

Approved Refiners: Names as listed on the DGCX Web site

Approved Vaults: Names as listed on the DGCX Web site

Delivery Period: First through sixth delivery day of the delivery month

First Notice Day: Business day immediately preceding first delivery day

Last Notice Day: Business day immediately preceding sixth delivery day

Delivery Process: Compulsory delivery as allocated by the Exchange on a random basis

Vault Charges: Rates applicable as published on the DGCX Web site

Delivery Instrument: Dubai Gold Receipt (i.e., Standard DGR along with validated refiner's certificate or CMI-Certified DGR only)

The calculation to convert this to a loco London price is considerably easier than for the three previous exchanges since there is no currency, purity, or weight factor to take into account—the quoted unit is U.S. dollars per troy ounce—so it is done in the same way as for the New York Mercantile Exchange (NYMEX):

$$((\text{Loco London Spot Gold Price} \times \text{Gold Forward Rate})/360) \times \text{Day Count to Delivery Day}$$

This would then represent the Exchange of Futures for Physicals (EFP), which would need to be subtracted from the exchange price to obtain an equivalent loco London spot equivalent.

New York Mercantile Exchange (United States)

There is, as yet, no widely followed gold exchange in Europe. Instead there is a leap in the exchanges that goes from Asia (where TOCOM remains the most important) to New York—trading in Europe is predominantly OTC.

On its Web site (www.nymex.com) the New York Mercantile Exchange, Inc. defines itself as "the world's largest physical commodity futures exchange and the preeminent trading forum for energy and precious metals. The gold contract is available for trading via open out-cry on the COMEX Division of the Exchange as well as electronically on CME Globex®.

"The Exchange has stood for market integrity and price trans-parency for more than 135 years. Transactions executed on the Exchange avoid the risk of counterparty default because the NYMEX clearinghouse acts as the counterparty to every trade. Trading is con-ducted in energy, metals, softs, and environmental commodity futures and options via the CME Globex® electronic trading system, open outcry, and NYMEX ClearPort®."

This exchange has yet another set of contract specifications. NYMEX defines these as:

Trading Unit: 100 troy ounces.

Price Quotation: U.S. dollars and cents per troy ounce.

Trading Hours: Open outcry trading is conducted from 8:20 a.m. until 1:30 p.m. (All times are Eastern Standard time.) Electronic trading is conducted from 6:00 p.m. until 5:15 p.m. via the CME Globex® trading platform, Sunday through Friday. There is a 45-minute break each day between 5:15 p.m. (current trade date) and 6:00 p.m. (next trade date). Off-exchange transactions can be submitted solely for clearing to the NYMEX ClearPort® clearing Web site.

Trading Months: Trading is conducted for delivery during the current calendar month; the next two calendar months; any February, April, August, and October falling within a 23-month period; and any June and December falling within a 60-month period beginning with the current month.

Minimum Price Fluctuation: 0.10 (10¢) per troy ounce ($10 per contract).

Last Trading Day: Trading terminates at the close of business on the third to last business day of the maturing delivery month.

Delivery: Gold delivered against the futures contract must bear a serial number and identifying stamp of a refiner approved and listed by the Exchange. Delivery must be made from a depository licensed by the Exchange.

Rules and Provisions: Complete delivery rules and provisions are detailed in Chapter 113 of the Exchange Rulebook.

Delivery Period: The first delivery day is the first business day of the delivery month; the last delivery day is the last business day of the delivery month.

Exchange of Futures for Physicals (EFP): The buyer or seller may exchange a futures position for a physical position of equal quantity. EFPs may be used to either initiate or liquidate a futures position.

Grade and Quality Specifications: In fulfillment of each contract, the seller must deliver 100 troy ounces (± 5 percent) of refined gold, assaying not less than .995 fineness, cast either in one bar or in three one-kilogram bars, and bearing a serial number and identifying stamp of a refiner approved and listed by the Exchange. A list of approved refiners and assayers is available from the Exchange upon request.

Position Accountability Levels and Limits: Any one month/all months: 6,000 net futures equivalent, but not to exceed 3,000 in the spot month.

Margin Requirements: Margins are required for open futures positions.

Trading Symbol: GC

Once again we are looking at U.S. dollars per troy ounce and for gold of 995 fine, which makes the rough guide calculations somewhat easier.

For traders looking to arbitrage the COMEX gold contract against London gold, the calculation is very simple. Essentially it is assumed that the two locations are absolutely fungible. Thus at its simplest, it is just the outright forward gold contango for each month that is the underlying calculation (below)—given the ease of converting 400-ounce bars to 100-ounce bars, particularly as they happen to be the same purity, and the large number of flights between London and New York. However, and as with all these exchanges above, the simple assumptions inherent in the calculation will vary on the basis of local conditions. To take a dramatic example, if all flights between the United Kingdom and the United States were grounded then clearly the EFP will be impacted, as the arbitrage would no longer be operational.

In general though, gold trades actively on COMEX for the February, April, June, August, and December contracts; the October contract is normally skipped in terms of the "active" month (the front month contract with the most open interest).

Thus, if the date today was September 1, then the active contract would be December. The theoretical EFP should be:

$$((\text{Loco London Spot Gold Price} \times \text{Gold Forward Rate}) / 360)$$
$$\times \text{Day Count to December } 1 = (((\$975 \times 2.50\%)/360) \times 91)$$
$$= 6.16 \text{ as a mid-rate.}$$

Therefore a market maker might well quote $6.05/6.25. Just to reiterate, this is the theoretical rate and not where it necessarily might be trading; instead it gives a rough guide.

·◦] Online Exchanges [◦··

TOCOM is, by its charter, an online exchange, whereas NYMEX started life as open outcry and has supplemented this business with its online activities. It is the extended trading hours provided by the latter that has seen its relevance and volumes increase even further.

Whereas Europe has always been primarily an OTC market, the reach of the CME Globex® trading platform has meant that Asian and European market makers have added this to their armory of risk management tools.

⋅⊰ A Health Warning! ⊱⋅

In each instance, these calculations can only be rule of thumb and are, at best, no more than an approximation. Outside the straight mathematical value suggested by these formulae, there may be local conditions that see the EFP (the differential between the cash and futures market) trade very differently in practice to where it should theoretically and for far longer than might be supposed.

While matters should ultimately correct, it may not be before a trader has lost either his or her job or a considerable amount of money—or both.

It is also worth noting that in each case I have provided rough calculations to convert somewhat esoteric sounding contracts (perhaps none more so than Hong Kong dollars per tael) back to a loco London format. However, for many individuals this is not even relevant as their entire exposure, or interest, to gold is in yuan or yen per gram, etc., and thus the arbitrage is immaterial.

Exchange-Traded Funds (ETFs)

What Is an ETF?

 The ETF is a relatively new feature of the precious metals markets. A definition, which is provided on www. ishares.com (ishares is the brand name that Barclays Global Investors, BGI, uses for its family of exchange-traded funds) is that an "ETF is an investment vehicle that combines key features of traditional mutual funds and individual stocks. ETFs are open-ended funds which like index mutual funds represent portfolios of securities that track specific indexes. A distinct difference is that ETFs trade like stocks and can be bought and sold (long or short) on an exchange and can employ the same trading strategies used with stocks."

More specifically gold ETFs are designed to track the price of gold, less the storage and administrative costs, and are backed, in most cases, by physical allocated gold.

Why a Gold ETF?

The key motivation for launching gold ETFs was to open up the gold market to a broader range of investors. The primary target being "real money funds" (pension funds, etc.) who might have been attracted to the notion of buying gold but who previously had no route to do so, perhaps being forbidden under the terms of their mandates from owning something that could not be pigeon-holed as either a bond or an equity or even simply that it might be illegal for these types of institutions to have direct owner-ship of a commodity. Similarly it would allow retail investors a relatively simple, and cheap, avenue in which to invest in gold.

Clearly, mining shares did fall under such a potential remit of the fund industry, as well as being accessible to small investors, but given the vagaries of geology, safety, records, hedge books, management ability, etc., then this would not necessarily have given real money direct exposure to gold.

At the time the detractors pointed out that the sheer numbers involved made it unlikely that pension funds would ever have the interest in owning gold as a diversifier to their overall portfolios. With an industry that has an estimated $2.6 trillion under management of defined benefit then clearly even 1 percent would lead to some 812 tonnes of gold being bought on a basis of $1,000 as the spot gold price—something that seems unlikely given that it is about one-third of the gold that is mined each year and clearly a 1-percent holding does not count as diversification.

Interestingly this is somewhat similar to the argument as to why sov-ereign wealth funds and central banks would not buy gold. In both instances there has been much speculation, but little hard evidence, that these types of institutions have invested in gold either by ETFs or via the underlying metal itself, outside the existing holdings of central banks.

The first ETF for gold was launched by Gold Bullion Securities in Sydney during March 2003, followed by London Gold Bullion Securities (now LyxOr Gold Bullion Securities) nine months later, and then in a variety of other locations. However, it was only with the advent of the New York listings that volumes really accelerated.

The first and largest—there is a correlation—ETF to be launched in the United States was streetTRACKS Gold Shares, which debuted in November 2004. In May 2008, it was renamed SPDR Gold Shares, and its Web site is www.spdrgoldshares.com.

Exchange-Traded Funds (ETFs)

This launch was followed in January 2005 by the Comex Gold Trust (IAU) (see www.ishares.com/product_info/fund/overview/IAU.htm). At the time of writing, SPDR has over 630 tonnes of gold in trust, and there is a further 67 tonnes or so in COMEX Gold Trust, plus smaller amounts in the other vehicles (London, Johannesburg, and so on). For Figure 8–1 I had thought to include the Indian ETFs for completeness, but there has been a debate as to whether Indian ETFs are truly representative, since they do not require the gold to be allocated in all cases. The overall interest in Indian ETFs has also been very small. Indeed there are so many different, tiny ETFs that the picture can become muddled.

However, there is little doubt that the cynics were wrong with the rapid growth in the concept—illustrated below—and also the absolute tonnages, with the U.S. ETFs, at the time of writing, holding some 700 tonnes of gold.

In Figure 8–1, which follows, please note that for the sake of clarity I have omitted 10 of the small ETFs, including only the three largest funds. The balances that the 10 smaller funds have accumulated do little to enhance the overall picture of investment and instead would only serve to make the chart rather more confusing. The cumulative total of the three ETFs shown is 758.04 tonnes, which is roughly 120 tonnes less than the total, had all 13 ETFs been included. However, the missing, smaller ETFs have tended to remain virtually static after their initial investment and have not shown the degree of fluctuation, and interest, of the three funds displayed, and I am more interested in illustrating the basic trend rather than the overall numbers.

If the Exchange-Traded Funds' total holdings of gold were compared to those of central banks, then they would rank in seventh place ahead of Japan, only falling behind the large traditional holders of the United States, the IMF, Germany, Italy, France, and Switzerland.

However, it is worth noting that the changes in the balances held in gold ETFs are likely to be considerably more volatile than the holdings of central banks and, depending on markets, could see further inflow or falls over time.

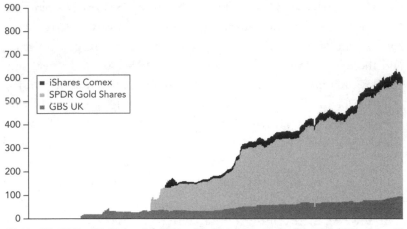

Figure 8-1

Largest Physical Gold-Backed Exchange-Traded Funds

(Amount of Gold Held in Tonnes)

Sources: Exchange-Traded Gold, SPDR®, iShares, Barclays Capital

⸾ Allocated Gold ⸾

Another attraction for many investors is that the ETF gold is allocated. That is to say that the gold held by these companies is readily identifiable in the vaults by its serial numbers rather than being part of an amorphous mass, which means the gold is the property of the fund and not a claim against the custodian (in the unlikely event that they were to go bust).

Pictures on the SPDR Web site (www.spdrgoldshares.com) show its executives posing by some of the gold that the company owns. It is noted that: "Gold Shares represent fractional, undivided beneficial ownership interests in the Trust, the sole assets of which are gold bullion, and, from time to time, cash. Gold Shares are intended to lower a large number of the barriers, preventing investors from using gold as an asset allocation and trading tool. These barriers have included the logistics of buying, storing and insuring gold. In addition, certain pension funds and mutual funds do not or cannot hold physical commodities, such as gold, or the derivatives." I have already described the barriers to ownership faced by some types of funds, but also in the paragraph preceding is the information that the shares represent beneficial ownership in the trust. Rather than owning the gold itself, the investors own a company that owns gold—the original notion was that investors would own the gold itself. However, this ran into both logistical and regulatory difficulties. It is difficult to argue, though, that this has in any way hampered its success.

·⊰ SPDR Gold Shares ⊱·

A quick glance at the press will give the latest valuation of the shares. This does not seem to correspond exactly to the gold price, which such valuations are supposed to mimic—even taking into account that they represent one-tenth of an ounce of gold. However, the definition of GLD (provided by the stock exchange) provides the answer:

Name: SPDR Gold Shares

Objective: Designed to track the price of gold
(net of Trust expenses)

Symbol: GLD

Exchange: New York Stock Exchange Arca

Initial Pricing: Based on the price of 1/10th of an ounce
of gold

Estimated Expense: 0.40%*

* The Sponsor and the Marketing Agent have agreed to reduce the fees payable to them from the assets of the Trust to the extent required so that the estimated ordinary expenses of the trust do not exceed an amount equal to 0.40% per annum of the daily net asset value during the period ending seven years from the date of the Trust Indenture or upon the earlier termination of the Marketing Agent Agreement. Investors should be aware that if the value of the Trust assets is less than approximately $388 million, the ordinary expenses of the Trust will be accrued at a rate greater than 0.40% per year of the daily ANAV of the Trust even after the Sponsor and the marketing Agent have completely reduced their combined fees of 0.30% per year of the daily ANAV of the Trust. This amount is based on the estimated ordinary expenses of the Trust.

Minimum Order Size: 1 share

Sponsor: World Gold Trust Services LLC

Trustee: Bank of New York

Custodian: HSBC Bank USA

Marketing Agent: State Street Global Markets, LLC, an affiliate of State Street Global Advisors

Short Sale Eligible?: Yes

Margin Eligible?: Yes

Structure: Continuously offered, open-ended investment trust.

Thus each share will represent smaller fractions of the original one-tenth ounce of gold over time; currently (April 2008) the figure is 0.098683 of an ounce of gold. As the World Gold Council says, "The expenses of administering the GLD Trust are accrued daily so that every investor pays a fair share, and that a tiny quantity of the gold backing the shares is sold every month to meet those expenses. This means that the amount of gold backing each share is reduced over time, but it is an extremely gradual process of erosion. Full details are published on the Trust's Web site."

While some small investors will prefer to invest via physical owner-ship of gold or perhaps mining equities, the simplest way is almost undoubtedly via ETFs and almost certainly why the World Gold Council (a marketing organization funded by leading mining compa-nies; please see the FAQs) has been so active in the setting up and pro-motion of this investment vehicle for gold.

9

Physical Gold

 For some people all gold is physical; the only type of gold that matters is the actual bars rather than the unallocated accounts and amorphous mass that is generally transacted. Therefore, in this chapter I would like to discuss "physical demand"—the generic term that market makers tend to use when they are besieged by customers asking for prices in anywhere from 500 ounces to a few thousand, usually from banks based in the Middle East and Asia but more specifically in Dubai, Hong Kong, Singapore, and so on.

For most people in the West, the notion of basing jewelry purchases—for that is still what nearly three-quarters of gold is destined to become—on the price of the metal remains rather unusual. The purchase of a wedding ring is not delayed until a suitable pullback in the price, nor is a bracelet sold because the price has rallied. However, the whole concept of gold purchases and sales has a very different connotation for much of the world.

⊰ Lining Up to Buy Gold ⊱

The first difference in the way that gold is viewed outside the West is the way in which the pieces themselves are displayed.

Generally, instead of price tags each piece will carry a label that gives its fine gold content, or even gross weight and purity. Although in most jurisdictions the purity is likely to be at least 90 percent rather than the 75 percent (18 carat) that is used for high quality jewelry in the West. It is even less likely to be the 9 carat—less than 40-percent gold—that is sometimes used and still with a label proclaiming it to be "pure 9 carat gold"—a confusion of terms in my opinion.

In Asia and the Middle East the pieces are generally marked with the weight, and there is typically a display on the wall that has an updated gold price, the offer price, plus a small markup for manufacture and profit. If this still sounds somewhat odd, then let me use a personal anecdote to illustrate the point. When I was getting married in Hong Kong, I visited the jewelers to buy wedding rings. For my (now) wife there was no problem as they had a ring that fit. Unfortunately they were going to have to make one for me; no problem. We went through all the usual rigmarole over size, thickness, purity, etc. It would be ready in a week. Final question: "Do you want today's metal price or do you want it on the day that you pick it up?" Not the sort of question that tends to get asked in Tiffany's! Being a little bullish I opted for the former—right choice as it rallied $5 over the next seven days.

A little fatuous perhaps but true and indicative of how different the concept is in different parts of the world. I saw examples of this many times during my six years in Hong Kong. I am still astounded by the lines that I used to see form outside jewelers following sharp falls in the gold price. Although the general rule from a trading point of view is that physical demand does not kick in until the price has stabilized at lower levels, the mentality being that it can always fall further, and the demand often waits until the price has started to tick higher again.

Different Cultures, Different Rationales

Second, the rationale behind buying gold jewelry is different between cultures. From a Western perspective jewelry is generally purchased for special occasions, with a wedding ring or engagement ring really the only time when it is considered a necessity to buy precious metals. Personally I detest going into a jewelry shop in the West, where it often seems that the attitude is that you are fortunate to be allowed in past the security gates let alone to have the temerity to inspect the pieces. A gross generalization I accept, but given my trade I should feel extremely blasé at the process, so if it makes me feel uncomfortable, then I am sure that the feeling is magnified for a great many other people.

In Asia I have few such qualms, and the process is much more egalitarian; besides there are any number of occasions when it is necessary to give a gift of gold. Indian wedding ceremonies are one of the most well-known examples, with the bride bedecked in gold jewelry that is her own property. It is still the case in some rural areas that the only wealth that a woman can own is her jewelry, but this used to be far more widely spread throughout Indian society.

Similarly, in Chinese society gold is given at weddings (mainly in the form of bangles) as well as occasions such as the birth of a child. Again I believe a personal anecdote can help here, as the concept seems rather alien to Western society. Both my children were born in Hong Kong. On their birth, friends and relatives of my (Chinese) wife arrived with gifts, including gold bracelets, necklaces, and medallions, whereas the Westerners produced a succession of toys and stuffed animals. Indeed, the whole event may sound rather disproportionate, with the Chinese perhaps being overly generous. However, such is the difference in the pricing of gold jewelry between East and West that the outlay was not that dissimilar.

Admittedly the children were not exactly enthused with the gold as infants, even when it showed pigs surfing or oxen skateboarding, an attempt to make their Chinese birth symbols more relevant to a child. Indeed there has been a growing preference for the Year of the Rat to be represented by a mouse, albeit the world's most famous mouse—Mickey. However, over 10 years later the gold gifts are locked away safely, long after many of the toys have been thrown away in the trash.

In most instances, this preference for gold has its roots locked in survival. The storage of wealth stems from a traditional need to provide for the future and to guard against tough times. Similarly to the purchase, the lack of sentimentality can be seen in the disposal of gold. To many in the West, every piece of jewelry is something to be treasured; the notion of trading in an old (perhaps broken) piece against the purchase of something new and more fashionable does not occur. I cannot imagine the reaction of my local London jewelers if I were to try to barter an old piece of jewelry against the purchase of a new one. However, this notion of "scrap" is key when looking at gold data and at its simplest partially explains the wide gap between new supply (from mines) and demand.

Consignment Stocks

In a perfect, simple world the customer would walk into a jewelry shop intending to buy a one-ounce piece of pure gold jewelry. A quick glance at the screen would show that the shop's selling price at that particular time was $1,000. Money would change hands, and the customer would leave the store satisfied. However, the retailer still has an outstanding short position that needs to be covered. With a quick call to their bullion bank, they would buy the ounce of gold, thus locking in their profit margin.

If only. At least from the jeweler's point of view, I cannot begin to imagine the reaction of the traders I know should they be asked for the prices of such small quantities. There is also the question of where the gold used in the manufacture of jewelry comes from in the first place.

Instead of this overly simplistic version described previously, banks will engage in their usual business of lending working capital. In this instance, the "funds" provided are in the form of gold bars rather than cash. As discussed in Chapter 2 on refining, the purities will differ for various markets and in accordance with the customary expectations of the local population and taking into account the capabilities of local jewelers. Some manufacturers need to take 9999 (four nines) kilo bars rather than 9999 large bars (400 ounces) because that is the largest size their machines can process as they chop, melt, and alter the purity.

Essentially, the banks lend gold to jewelers and to manufacturers (who may not necessarily be the same entity, but let's assume that they are for greater ease). These companies then draw down the loans and pay them back (by buying gold and remitting U.S. dollars) as they see fit and depending on market circumstances. The terms of these loans will clearly vary with the creditworthiness of the customer and the overall market "tightness" (shorthand for the cost of credit, nearby interest rates, and the availability of the required bar types).

Thus a large, well-financed manufacturer might be allowed to take a consignment free of interest payments as long as the gold is to be used within a set time frame (two weeks, for example). It would repay the loan by buying the gold at the loco London spot price, plus a pre-agreed-upon premium for the bar purity, size, and location. Conversely, a small company would be given a much smaller amount of gold—perhaps even just a kilo—and would be expected to pay for a large proportion of this in advance.

Given that the search for profits is eternal, the jewelers and/or manufacturers will usually try to increase their margins by trading gold, such as buying in advance of a key gift-giving season perhaps. Or if they are generally bullish or bearish about the prospects for gold, they may go long by locking in prices in advance of anticipated price increases, or conversely they may delay purchases if they believe that prices are likely to fall.

·᛫᛬᷊ Gold as a Gift ᛫᷊·

The key gold-giving occasions are:

Lunar New Year: The major Chinese celebration falling between late January and late February

Akshaya Thrithiya: Indian festival falling in April or May

Diwali: Start of the Indian (Hindu) New Year in October or November

Indian Wedding Season: Running from late September to late December

Eid al Fitr: Muslim festival marking the end of Ramadan

Eid al Adha: Muslim festival occurring the day after the ending of the Hajj pilgrimage

I have not given exact dates for these festivals, since they are determined by lunar calendars and vary from year to year. Additionally, certain other signals—mainly astrological—can count for or against the dates. For example, according to the Chinese, certain years are very propitious for getting married and/or having children. A dragon year—which happens once every 12 years—is seen as particularly lucky; thus weddings and births will surge. The converse can be true for some months during certain years; the ghost month (the seventh of the lunar year) is not particularly popular, for example.

However, while these events are key for the overall physical off-take for a given year, they will not necessarily have an impact in a given month because the retailers will look to position themselves ahead of the anticipated buying (or slowing up ahead of the ghost month), and in the case of an Indian girl, her parents may start accumulating the gold at birth rather than waiting until an announcement of marriage. Thus both buyers and sellers look to take advantage of market movements.

For all the thoughts about gold as a ready store of value, about it being a panacea in uncertain times, its greatest use remains as jewelry. Although, admittedly, the notion of jewelry does vary; someone who buys a necklace at Tiffany's may have an entirely different motive from someone who buys a piece containing a similar amount of metal in Asia. Possibly it may be that the tax is different for buying adornment gold as opposed to investment metal in a particular country, and thus buying jewelry is simply much more cost-efficient than buying a small bar.

ᵉᵢ Scrap Metal ᵢₑ

In the West, it is often felt that it is not entirely proper to sell jewelry that you have bought or been given. Indeed, generally why would you? The bracelet that you, in the West, bought for $1,000 might only have $500 of gold in it, which might be a generous estimate since markups can be anything up to 500 percent. Therefore, selling it for the scrap metal value is no way to recoup your investment. Besides, the piece was probably bought for a special occasion and now holds as much sentimental as monetary value.

However, and as before, there is little such sentimentality attached to the metal in other areas of the world—and swapping the jewelry for a more up to date piece makes perfect sense if the difference is only a few (not a few hundred) dollars.

Scrap is an extremely important component of the annual gold supply, second only to mining and roughly double that for official sector sales. Indeed, GFMS estimate scrap flows of 955.6 tonnes for 2007, with 285.8 tonnes coming from the Middle East and a further 237.1 tonnes from East Asia. In contrast the U.S. supplied just 84 tonnes of scrap gold.

The greatest outpouring of scrap that I ever witnessed was during the Asian financial crisis of the late 1990s. This was a period when several countries saw a meltdown in the value of their currencies. Given that gold is denominated in U.S. dollars, its value in local currency terms increased substantially as regional economies were hit, dramatically underlining why the population had bought gold in the first place. To maintain purchasing power, much of this gold was then sold into the market. In some cases, national pride saw gold donated to the country to enable the hard-hit governments to sell the metal and raise much needed U.S. dollars.

Gold: Myths and Reality

 The task of explaining the many properties ascribed to gold to an alien would not be easy. The conversation could probably start off fairly easily, explaining that a single ounce can be drawn into 50 miles of thin gold wire or beaten into a sheet covering almost 100 square feet … truly remarkable.

As for its use in jewelry, because gold does not become dull and can be found as yellow, rose, or white (depending on what it is alloyed with), it is again an incredible metal. By undergoing special processes, green and purple gold can be created too.

However, trying to explain gold's role as a refuge in times of upheaval, its historic inflation-busting qualities, and as a store of value, the conversation is likely to become rather more difficult. At its worst it could degenerate into a conversation akin to one with an inquisitive six year old where every explanation that you flounder to give is met with the one-word answer "Why?"

History

I said at the start of the book that if anyone was interested in why the Incas had gold or the Egyptians fashioned their most valued pieces out of the metal, then this was not the right book to buy. This is where I recant very slightly, although only in passing.

The fact is that gold is an inescapable part of human history. It has been valued through millennia for its ability to shine, for its workability, and for its scarcity. In the past its use was often reserved for royalty, nobility, and items of religious significance. In some societies its color is associated with deities. This history has translated to its near mythical status over the sum of human existence.

Doubtless in the Stone Age a weapon made of stone was highly valued, whereas in the Bronze and Iron Ages it would have lost much of its value. Today few stones are seen as mythical; certainly flint is not near the top of anyone's "must have" list. However, gold has never been an everyday item, and it is this exclusivity that has been preserved throughout the ages—so much so that it is part of language and of our psyche.

At the Olympics athletes strive for gold medals, the pinnacle of achievement in their chosen sport; soccer-playing nations compete for the World Cup (made out of gold of course); winners of Nobel prizes receive a gold medal to recognize their contribution to humankind. We acknowledge the preeminence of gold when talking about silence being "golden" or living out our "golden years." Retailers and advertisers try to cash in on this connotation by promising us "gold credit cards," "Gold Blend" coffee, "All Gold" chocolates. A quick trawl through Google for "gold and food" gives you dog food, fish food, baby food, and so on. None of them contain gold, hopefully, but it is presumably believed that by linking these products with gold we believe that we are buying a premium product and are special ourselves. Indeed, Sigmund Freud commented, "Our fascination with gold is related to the fantasies of early childhood."

⋅⊰ Gold as a Diversifier ⊱⋅

With the growth in commodities as an asset class, banks have conducted a number of studies assessing the appropriate percentage of this sector to provide the optimal Sharpe Ratio for a portfolio.

However, there has been little independent published research on gold in a portfolio by the largest holders of gold—the central banks.

Possibly the only publicized views have been those of the European Central Bank when selecting 15 percent in gold upon establishing the ECB (though I feel that has rather more to do with the ownership of its constituent members at the time) and of Ms. Maria Gueguina of the Central Bank of Russia, who, in her theoretical comments to an LBMA Conference (covered in Chapter 4), saw 10 percent as the correct percentage of gold in that country's central bank's reserves.

The World Gold Council has commissioned a number of surveys showing the benefits that gold can bring to a portfolio. In one such study for U.S. institutional investors called *Gold as a Strategic Asset* (Richard Michaud, Robert Michaud, and Katharine Pulvermacher, 2006), the authors conclude, "Gold may have a comparable portfolio weight to asset classes such as small cap and emerging markets due to its value as a diversifying asset. A strategic allocation to gold is dependent on portfolio risk level. We find a small though significant allocation of 1 to 2 percent at low risk and 2 to 4 percent in a balanced portfolio. While not statistically significant at high risk levels, gold may provide stability in poor markets and economic climates to long-term institutional strategic investors." See Figure 10–1.

As a rough guide, taking the start of the subprime woes and the credit crunch as of August 2007, gold would have been an excellent addition to any portfolio. In that period of time, it has risen from $660 to a high of $1,030; and, most tellingly, since this was not simply a result of the decline in the dollar, it rose from 485 euros to 665 euros.

·≈[Gold as a Store of Value]≈·

Portable Wealth

This description encompasses gold's role as both a way in which it lends itself to being portable wealth and as a possible long-term hedge against inflation.

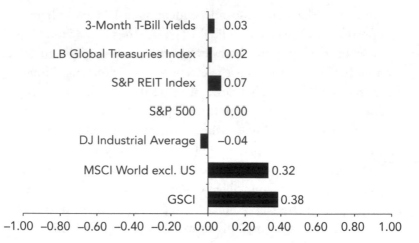

Figure 10–1
**United States: Five-Year Correlation of Weekly Returns on
Key Asset Classes and Gold (in U.S. Dollars)**

Sources of data: Global Insight, World Gold Council, Lehman Brothers

Probably the most recent example of gold representing a large-scale store of wealth in helping refugees was during the Vietnam War and its aftermath. Portions of the population fled in leaky boats, taking their family's money with them in the form of bars, coins, and jewelry, and in some instances it was alleged that they fled with the tacit approval of the government, which allowed them to leave in the crowded vessels on payment of 10 ounces of gold per person. The metal that they were left with was intended to help them start their new lives abroad. It seems that this strategy worked reasonably well with the gold being readily convertible into cash.

By association, in the run-up to Hong Kong being handed back to China in June 1997, some comments in the international financial press suggested that the local population would be wise to convert their available assets to gold in the event that they had to take to the high seas. Living in Hong Kong at the time as I was, this was an argument that made as little sense then as it does now. I held my account with a major international bank; I knew, should the situation take a turn for the worse, rather than buy gold and look around for a small boat, I would simply ask the bank to open an account in London, New York, Tokyo, or the like, and transfer the money there for me. A few years later now, I could pretty much accomplish the same thing through my online banking account.

Hong Kong is clearly very much a first world country. This notion of gold as a store of value makes more sense in places where the banking system is not so developed, such as for the refugees of Darfur (if they had the money) or perhaps rural India, where a distrust of the banking system still exists.

Indeed in the months following the Asian tsunami of December 2004, the Indian state of Tamil Nadu, one of the most urbanized regions, saw an upsurge in gold buying as survivors used their relief money to hold their savings in gold until such a time as it could be used in reconstruction.

However, as societies come to trust more in financial institutions, this feature must surely diminish in importance. Indeed the recent rally in the gold price was partly born out of distrust for the state of the global financial system as investors sought a safe haven for their assets.

The Inflation Fighter

As for inflation, there is an old anecdote that a sovereign coin (a U.K. gold coin with a metal content of just under a quarter of an ounce) has always been enough to buy dinner at the Savoy Hotel in London. Currently the Royal Mint Web site tells me that I can buy a sovereign for £145, which, had the Savoy not been closed for refurbishment, would cover the £100 or so per head nicely. Thus, the point is proved, although not very scientifically!

If you are more fashion oriented, then perhaps the idea that an ounce of gold has always been enough to buy a respectable outfit might fit rather better. The World Gold Council has found supporting evidence of this theory by comparing the cost of clothing from medieval England, through to the 1700s, and finally today ($1,000 or so being a welcome addition to the clothes budget).

However, to switch back to food once more, then an extremely long-term example can be found in Stephen Harmston's *Gold as a Store of Value* (World Gold Council Research Study number 22, November 1998), which states: "It is said that an ounce of gold bought 350 loaves of bread in the time of Nebuchadnezzar, king of Babylon, who died in 562 B.C. The same ounce of gold still buys approximately 350 loaves of bread today. Across 2,500 years gold has in other words retained its purchasing power, relative to bread at least, and has had a real rate of return of zero."

Gold as a modern "inflation buster" probably dates from the gold standard because it was the mechanism whereby banks were kept "honest" and were only able to print notes backed by sufficient metal. Much of the evidence of the long-term historical efficacy of gold in this respect is anecdotal. However, when looking at gold more recently, the picture is not quite so simple. The chart below shows the gold price plotted against inflationary expectations, the latter being the yield on the 10-year U.S. government bond relative to the yield on the 10-year U.S. government bond that is inflation indexed.

Indeed, gold has underperformed inflationary expectations over the last decade except for the last year, which I see as being a combination of three factors: the first being that there have been new instruments to help guard against the inflationary threat, the second being that inflation has been ticking along at low levels, and the third being that gold was a relatively neglected investment. See Figure 10–2.

The timing of gold's outperformance is significant because it coincides with gold finding renewed favor with investors.

I believe that this trend shows that it comes down to a trust in the monetary authorities or the banking system. Trust them and you don't need gold, but if that confidence is misplaced, then these traditional attributes start to look far more attractive, which is particularly true when there are now a myriad of ways to protect oneself against inflation.

Indeed, Barclays Capital has commented: "While gold, energy and other commodities respond well in inflationary times, the most efficient way to hedge inflation is, logically, via the inflation-linked markets. Over the last decade the trading of inflation has become

Gold: Myths and Reality

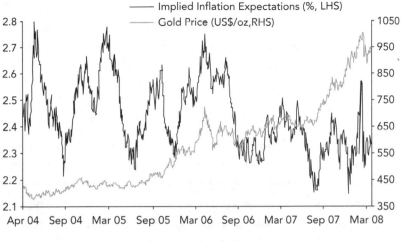

Figure 10–2

Gold Prices versus Implied Inflation Expectations

Sources: EcoWin, Barclays Capital

more liquid, and consequently more popular. The easiest way to access inflation is via inflation-linked bonds, with Treasury Inflation Protected Securities (commonly referred to as TIPS) being bought by both institutional and retail investors. These bonds pay a fixed, real-rate coupon, based on a floating principal which accretes at the rate of inflation. At maturity the investor receives back the greater of either par or par plus the compounded inflation over the investment horizon.

"More sophisticated investors have turned to the derivative markets to mitigate their inflation-linked liabilities. Trading in CPI swaps and real-rate swaps has become commonplace in most developed markets globally, and emerging markets have seen the development of both cash and derivative markets. The use of derivatives allows for more bespoke solutions, versus the generic nature of TIPS investments. TIPS do have their advantages, however, with the floating rate element affording lower volatility and consequently making them a very attractive beta allocation for diversification as well as ALM/LDI purposes."

However, there will be some people who remain naturally suspicious of politicians and thus believe that gold's role is so central to the financial system that it is only by misleading the public that this role has been relinquished.

Gold Is Not a Dollar!

Several commodities can trade as a counter to the U.S. dollar but gold is far more correlated to the currency. Briefly this is because gold is priced in dollars but often bought by the general population of other countries, such as India, China, and so on. Therefore, when the U.S. dollar falls it is assumed that overseas investors will increase the amount that they purchase and therefore the price goes up to compensate.

At least that is the theory. In reality, the rationale is generally superfluous such that simply if the U.S. dollar falls then gold will almost always rise. Gold's general under- or overperformance in terms of the U.S. dollar is perhaps rather more important since it shows its relative performance compared to extraneous influences.

Additionally, for many people gold is simply a currency, and thus if the dollar falls, gold rises in the same way that the euro, yen, or pound does. It is very simple.

The consequences of this relationship are examined in more depth in the next chapter.

Conspiracy Theories

With gold maintaining a hold over our psyche it is unsurprising that it appears in so many conspiracy theories. Its anonymity and desirability only increases its mystique and hence its role in such stories and/or rumors.

In December 2000, a lawsuit was filed that alleged "manipulative activities in the gold market from 1994 to the present time orchestrated by government officials acting outside the scope of their legal or constitutional authority and certain large bullion banks active in over-the-counter gold derivatives markets and on the Commodities Exchange ("COMEX") in New York."

The defendants were a remarkable group:

1. The BIS or Bank for International Settlements, which is sometimes referred to as the "central banks' central bank."

2. Alan Greenspan, then chairman of the Board of Governors of the U.S. Federal Reserve System

3. William J. McDonough, then president of the Federal Reserve Bank of New York

4. J P Morgan & Co. Ltd.

5. Chase Manhattan Corp.

6. Citigroup Inc.

7. Goldman Sachs Group Inc.

8. Deutsche Bank AG

9. Lawrence H. Summers, then U.S. Secretary of the Treasury

The case was dismissed in the first quarter of 2002.

However, it seemed to be a common theme that the price of gold was languishing because of the activities of the politicians and complicit banks. The rationale for many of these was apparently that inflation was rampant, but to disguise this fact the price of gold needed to be kept artificially low to prevent the general public from working this out. Hence, U.S. president Bill Clinton (who seemed to figure in a number of the conspiracies) apparently issued an order that gold was to be released from Fort Knox to suppress the price. Unfortunately, though, the scale of the manipulation was such that rather than being a short-term operation, where the gold could simply be bought back quickly without anyone realizing it, the stocks held in Fort Knox (in excess of 8,000 tonnes) were actually all used up.

To overcome this hurdle (clearly the gold price still needed to be kept under control) the U.S. government sought the help of the Germans who agreed to lend their entire stock of gold for this purpose. Unfortunately this was not enough to stem the bubbling undercurrent of gold demand either, a total of 11,500 tonnes of gold, nearly five years of mine supply, and $368 billion (on a basis of $1,000 per ounce) or $110 billion (on a basis of $300) was wasted in a fruitless enterprise. The net result is that the vaults of both countries are empty.

An alternative to this story was that various countries lent their gold to bullion banks that promptly sold it. The currency raised was placed on deposit and when the gold price fell the gold would be bought back delivering a nice profit. Again, unfortunately, the gold price rose, leaving the banks with an enormous marked-to-market loss that threatened both the individual institutions as well as the global economy, so the matter was hushed up. Long Term Capital Management (LTCM) often figured in this particular scenario as well.

Apparently, the European central bank Gold Agreement (EcbGA), covered in Chapter 4, was not in fact a mechanism to remove uncertainty from the price, but rather served to provide a degree of certainty that central banks would act in concert to ensure that the price of gold could not rally.

Any person, or institution, that disagreed with this was automatically labeled as being part of the "cabal," the group that allegedly was brought together to prevent populations from discovering that inflation was in fact rampant. In a forerunner of the "Da Vinci Code" style of conspiracy, if a matter could not be sufficiently explained, it was sometimes suggested that "the Vatican" was the mystery lender or seller of gold.

The problem, as with all the best conspiracy theories, is that such matters are hard to disprove easily. For many of the defendants these would be nuisance allegations, not worth commenting on. Those that did bother to reply would probably content themselves with words such as "groundless" or "baseless." However, the rejoinder would probably echo the famous quip from Mandy Rice-Davies (in a real 1960s conspiracy) when she was asked why Lord Astor had denied even meeting her, let alone having had an affair: "Well, he would, wouldn't he?"

Gold: Myths and Reality

All I can say, having worked for four of the largest gold trading institutions in the world (and two of the five banks in the lawsuit mentioned above), is that I have never seen any evidence of governmental (quasi or otherwise) tampering in the gold market. I have helped many nations sell gold but have not sat on the trading desk with an enormous short position waiting for the phone to ring signaling help from the likes of President Clinton, Mr. Greenspan, Mr. Summers, and so on. Instead, if we had a large short position in a rising market, then it would have been with a degree of trepidation and hoping that the price fell again to enable us to at least cover our positions.

A more specific lawsuit was brought by Blanchard and Company Inc. of New Orleans—the largest retail dealer in physical gold in the United States—on behalf of themselves and their clients who had bought gold. The basic upshot of the charge was that JP Morgan and Barrick (the gold mining company) had colluded to suppress the price of gold at the expense of individual investors by use of its hedging program. Indeed the allegation was that given global growth in incomes the price should have been $740 an ounce in December 2002 rather than some $400 lower at that time.

In the end the case was settled out of court, with the charge against Morgan being dropped first and apparently Blanchard having to pay damages to Barrick after they countersued for libel in November 2005.

Probably the foremost organization alleging manipulation of the gold price is GATA, who describe themselves on their Web site (www.gata.org) as the "Gold Anti-Trust Action Committee ... organized in January 1999 to advocate and undertake litigation against illegal collusion to control the price and supply of gold and related financial securities." Despite the recent rise in gold to all-time record (nominal) highs, GATA believes that gold is still undervalued. In a full-page advertisement taken out in the *Wall Street Journal* in January 2008, they stated, among other things, that "The gold reserves of the United States have not been fully and independently audited for half a century. Now there is proof that those gold reserves and those of other Western nations are being used for the surreptitious manipulation of the international currency, commodity, equity, and bond markets....

The objective of this manipulation is to conceal the mismanagement of the U.S. dollar so that it might retain its function as the world's reserve currency. But to suppress the price of gold is to disable the barometer of the international financial system so that *all* markets may be more easily manipulated. This manipulation has been a primary cause of the catastrophic excesses in the markets that now threaten the whole world.

Gold's recent rise toward $900 per ounce shows that the price-suppression scheme is faltering. When it is widely understood how central banks have been suppressing gold, its price may rise to $3,000 or $5,000 or more."

The argument seems to have moved on from just the Clinton administration "manipulating" the gold price to a general concern about central banks and governments as a whole. I have met with 45 out of the world's 50 largest holders of gold in their own countries and have discussed the topic of gold reserve management with almost all 50 of these nations. Not once have I ever been asked how to prevent the rise of the price of gold. Not once have I ever had a discussion on gold being the bellwether of world financial health and how keeping the price low will bring benefits in other markets. Not once have I seen large gold orders placed by central banks to act as a lid on the gold price.

However, I have had many conversations on the most effective way to sell gold and to minimize market disruption. I have sat with political and financial leaders who believe that selling gold would be akin to disposing of a family heirloom. I have heard a senior central banker bemoaning that the low yields obtainable on gold reserves means that the central bank needs funds from the ministry of finance just to meet its running costs—politically very unpopular—and elsewhere was told by a central bank governor that even discussing mobilizing gold reserves could be enough to bring the government down.

So, yes, gold *is* sensitive; it is seen as a case entirely different from that of any other reserve asset—but is this a conspiracy? I think not. In fact, I know not.

⤙ Gold the Barometer ⤚

I do find myself agreeing with GATA, though, that gold can be a barometer of the global financial health. Whereas it could have been argued for much of the 1990s, and indeed for much of this millennium, that gold had lost its place as a major financial instrument, the recent turmoil in the currency and fixed income markets has rekindled interest in the metal as an investment and as an important financial instrument. This feature of gold is examined in more depth in the next chapter.

Gold at Record Highs

·≈[Record High to Nominal High]≈·

 It is impossible to predict where the price of gold will be trading by the time that this book is published. Indeed, if I could do so with any certainty, I would have given up my job many years ago and be happy to watch the world go by from the luxury of a comfortable chair in an exotic location. Instead I have to be content looking at the rationale for gold rallying from 19-year lows in 1999 to all-time nominal highs in 2008, as shown in Figure 11–1.

In early 2008 gold broke $850 for the first time since 1980 and then marched through $1,000 to register its all-time high. Admittedly this is only the highest ever price in nominal terms; in real terms I have seen the price listed anywhere between $1,960 and $2,370. A stunningly wide band shows that there is a multitude of different ways of demonstrating a "financial truth," in this instance depending on which inflation or deflator methodology is used, and perhaps providing some of the rationale for gold rallying as it did!

In 1980, gold rose to its heady heights on a combination of inflationary fears, the oil price, and the Russians having marched into Afghanistan. Silver was even more rampant, managing to reach some $49 per ounce in nominal terms, a level

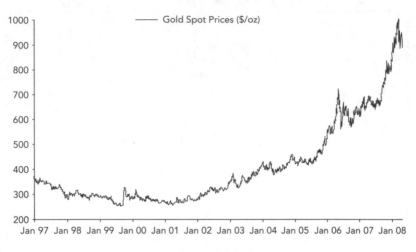

Figure 11-1

The Gold Price in U.S. Dollars, 1997–2008

Sources: EcoWin, Barclays Capital

that it has never seriously challenged since. In that environment of fear, energy rationing, and uncertainty, gold was the natural destination for investors.

However, by the late 1990s, it was clear that gold no longer resonated as a financial investment for the vast majority of people. The Cold War was over, energy prices were low, and in a world dominated by news of technological discoveries why would anyone be interested in such a low-tech opportunity? Besides, even the most solidly long term of all investors (central banks) were deserting it; Australia, Switzerland, and the U.K. had all sold, or at least announced their intention of doing so. The market was dominated by the hedging—accelerated selling—of the gold producers, and the war of words over who should take the blame for the demise of gold raged between the miners and the central banks.

Gold was so marginalized that it seemed little could be done to rescue it. Admittedly the European central banks had done their best to remove uncertainty by timetabling their selling and then various mining companies announced their intention not to hedge. However, by the time that the planes flew into the World Trade Center on 9/11, gold was still languishing. There was some hedge fund buying of gold that day but very little—few people had the appetite for much more than stunned horror anyway—and ultimately gold could not hold its gains.

During George W. Bush's reelection campaign in 2004 Al-Qaeda released a tape calling for fresh attacks on the United States. Political commentators were divided as to whether this was an election advantage for Bush or John Kerry. Currency markets were similarly split in their interpretation as to who would benefit. In this confusion the dollar did not move. Obviously, though, it was clearly bullish for gold: uncertainty, elections, attacks. However, such was the lack of confidence in the market that it could not even react to such a significant piece of news as it was simply wedded to the fate of the U.S. dollar. When that failed to react, gold could not overcome such an obstacle.

Therein lay the seeds of this recent rally. The consistent weakness of the U.S. currency has seen gold benefit, added to which the huge pools of investment money looking for new opportunities, commodities increasingly viewed as an acceptable asset class, a growing distrust in the infallibility of monetary authorities, and a desire for investments that are clear cut and simple to understand rather than being dependent on a fortunate set of outcomes or an abstruse branch of mathematics. Indeed these features plus some central banks being forced to cut interest rates in the face of one financial crisis after another, even while the media trumpet the return of inflation, all helped to create the perfect storm for gold.

Indeed, if asked for a shopping list of conditions to ensure a rally in gold, recent events have pretty much checked off every one.

·≈[Gold: The Quasi Currency]≈·

As I have commented previously, given that gold is quoted in dollars and primarily bought by non-dollar–domiciled individuals, then its price will tend to go up as the U.S. dollar falls. The assumption is that increased buying will come into the market and thus the price has to rise to maintain equilibrium. In a sense that is the "commodity" explanation for gold as a currency; which simply states that as the U.S dollar rises, then gold, by definition, must fall.

At least that is the theory. In reality, the rationale is generally superfluous, and, simply stated, if the U.S. dollar falls, then gold will almost always rise. An example of recent correlations is shown in Figures 11–2 and 11–3. While generally correlation is extremely high between gold and the euro (the currency most closely watched to gauge moves in gold), at times it has become nearly 1.00 (or perfectly correlated). Figure 11–2 shows the gold and the euro/ U.S. dollar exchange rate tracking one another reasonably closely since 2000.

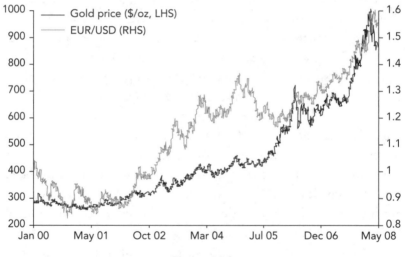

Figure 11-2

Price of Gold and Euro/U.S. Dollar, January 2000–May 2008

Sources: EcoWin, Barclays Capital

However, it is Figure 11–3 that is more interesting in many ways. This chart shows that the movements of the two are closely correlated at nearly 0.79; it is not the scale of the move but simply when either gold or the euro goes up so does the other one. To a purist this comparison might look to be nonsensical, since both are quoted against the

U.S. dollar. However, I believe it simply shows that gold's overriding driver is the U.S. dollar, and it is this relationship that traders spend the vast majority of their time watching. When they are bullish for gold and the euro-to-dollar exchange is rising, then gold will probably go up by a greater percentage, but by a smaller percentage when they are a bit more skeptical.

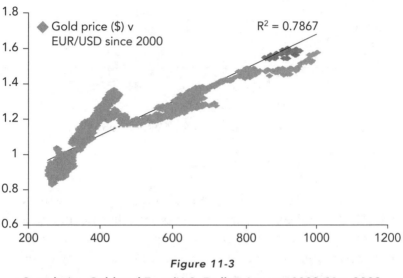

Figure 11-3

Correlating Gold and Euro/U.S. Dollar, January 2000–May 2008

Sources: EcoWin, Barclays Capital

However, this is not to say that gold exclusively follows the U.S. dollar. Indeed, Figure 11–4 shows gold in euro terms. As can be clearly seen, the metal has also risen substantially against this currency over the last few years. Indeed it is this rise that denotes gold's rally (in both U.S. dollars and euro terms) as being of its own making rather than simply a reaction to the sell-off in the U.S. dollar. Thus, while it is important to follow gold's performance in relation to the U.S. dollar, for a truer evaluation it is vital to view its record against other currencies (typically the euro), which should give a clearer picture of the metal's performance and market sentiment.

Figure 11-4
The Euro Gold Price, 1997–2008

Sources: EcoWin, Barclays Capital

For those new to the gold market, it does not operate in the same way as a standard commodity market or even like platinum. With other metals it is much more a case of supply and demand. For example, if a platinum smelter should be forced to close down because of problems, then prices will rise. Indeed concerns over the power supply to South Africa's platinum mines caused the metal to rally by over $700 in just one month in early 2008, a rise of some 45 percent.

While gold did move slightly higher in response to the same news, it was much more restrained. First and foremost, South Africa is not responsible for 80 percent of the world's gold supply, while it is the supplier for roughly this amount of the global primary supply of platinum (in the form of mined metal). It is no longer even the world's largest gold producer; according to GFMS, that honor belongs to China. Second, while there are no known large stockpiles of platinum, there are plenty for gold, in effect the reserves of the central banks or even Asian gold scrap, which can come onto the market at times when the price is high. Therefore, gold rarely, if ever, trades in accordance with usual supply-and-demand trends—imports falling in one country or rising in another—perhaps with an additional caveat, at least not for very long.

However, the market does look at "big picture" supply and demand, the large accumulation, or disposal, by central banks or the hedging intentions of gold mining companies.

So the market tends to ignore news headlines that Indian gold demand has moved higher or lower and will look to other stories on which to base its trading decisions. It is this characteristic of ignoring run-of-the-mill flows of metal that sets gold aside from other commodities and gives it its status as a quasi currency.

Undoubtedly though, the currency component is the most important long-term factor influencing gold prices. While inflation fears or changes in geopolitics may cause gold to under- or overperform against a variety of currencies, in the end it is the currency component that traders most often refer back to even if it is via a secondary route, i.e., gold might temporarily be very strongly correlated to oil, which in turn might be heavily correlated to the U.S. dollar.

Gold: The Quasi Commodity

The last few years have seen the emergence of commodities as an asset class. More banks have become market makers in this field, or even just white-labeling transactions, and there has been a rapid rise in the number of institutions offering commodity-linked products to their customer base—be they "real money" (pension funds) or leveraged investments (hedge funds and the like).

While gold shares some characteristics with commodities, it has often been included as part of the general argument for diversification, which has been central to the appeal of commodities as an asset class in particular and not correlated to fixed income or equities in particular. So while gold is a quasi currency, it is also a quasi commodity. However, one of the features that usually makes commodities particularly attractive for long-dated investment is that they have traditionally been backwardated, which is very different from the contango market that generally prevails for gold.

Backwardation allows for very attractive *trade optics*—the term used to describe how a trade looks to the eye without number crunching. For example, if the price of spot gold today is $975 and you are told that you can buy it for delivery in two years time for $1,050, then that does not sound nearly as attractive as being able to buy three-month copper (the standard delivery time is $8,500, yet you only have to pay $7,700 if you are prepared to wait two years). However, both are fair market prices. This scenario also means that the plethora of investment products that have been offered in commodities tend to use backwardated commodities wherever possible and have tended not to use gold, particularly where the general outlook is bullish as the "optics" look far more attractive.

Gold has not been ignored, however, as the psychological affinity that people have for it has led to its inclusion, by demand, in many structured products. This situation simply would not exist for other metals such as zinc or lead.

The Perception of Central Banks and Gold

The search for diversification and yield has seen hedge funds, pension funds, private banks, sovereign wealth funds, etc. all become involved in commodity markets. The assumption from many commentators has been that central banks are also closely involved in this hunt and therefore will turn to the (quasi) commodity that they know best—gold.

As mentioned in Chapter 4, it is received market wisdom that central banks are buying gold. If they are not actually buying gold, then they are developing strategies. If they are not developing strategies, it will only be a matter of time until they do. Indeed I have been told by portfolio managers at hedge funds that they "know for a fact that the Fed has ordered China to buy gold." The rationale was that at the time the Fed was trying to hike long-term rates but could not effectively do so when China was buying enormous quantities of U.S. government bonds; therefore the Chinese were supposedly being told that instead of buying U.S. paper, they had to buy gold. The fact that the math was not even vaguely equivalent didn't matter; perception was all important. Another example is the time when I read on a newswire that an analyst was claiming that a certain oil-producing nation was certain to buy gold; I dismissed it as nonsense but the market rallied. Why did I take such a high-handed attitude? Simple: The central bank of the country in question was selling gold to me at the time! All of which proves that it is not necessarily the particular properties or outlook for gold that is important but merely sentiment that can drive the price.

·⊸[Sentiment]⊸·

All markets are sentiment driven, at least partly. Anyone who has ever invested or traded will remember times when every piece of bad news was studiously ignored and each piece of good news was seized on as though it were etched in stone, until the time that this swings around by 180 degrees!

Gold reacts exactly in this way; in the late 1990s it was virtually impossible to find anyone who had a positive word to say about it, by 2007 it was the doomsayers who were in short supply. It is this type of trading activity that has sometimes led to gold being described as a postrationalization market. People buy it because they want to—they are not actually sure of the reason or at least cannot point to a single event that spurred them to it. Instead they buy it first and worry about the rationale later.

I remember having a conversation with the representative of a central bank as to why gold was rallying. He confidently told me that another bank had informed him that the Chinese yuan would be revalued that weekend, and hence the local population was buying gold in anticipation of this. Once the rumor hit the international markets, then professional investors were getting involved too.

Is this situation plausible? At first glance, without thinking about it, probably "yes." However, upon short reflection you realize that the answer is actually "no." In fact I pointed out that it was exactly the wrong way to look at it. If the Chinese believed that their currency was being revalued, it would mean fewer yuan per dollar. Therefore the price of any dollar-denominated asset, such as gold, would actually go down in local currency terms.

However, what was true was that market sentiment was positive, people wanted to buy and they needed a story to postrationalize their decision. This story seemed to fit in well and hence made the market feel comfortable with its decision. Just for the record, the yuan was not revalued that weekend. Although this is a true story, it is an extreme example. However, the notion of sentiment as a driver of direction is key.

Physical Demand versus Investment Demand

While headlines on supply and demand, particularly as related to gold imports or consumption figures, do not generally affect gold prices, physical demand has been the bedrock of the gold market for centuries.

Although it may appear as jewelry rather than investment in statistics—simply because different tax structures may make it more sensible to sell the metal as an adornment rather than as a lump—historically this is where most gold is destined to end up. According to figures produced by GFMS, world jewelry consumption was 2,401 tonnes in 2007—up from 2,284 the previous year but considerably below the 3,204 tonnes recorded in 2000. This change is easily detected in identifiable investment, which GFMS sees as 654 tonnes in 2007, up from 165 tonnes in 2000.

However, with gold prices at record highs the newswires have been full of headlines such as these selections from Reuters: "India gold demand falls as prices stay firm," or "Italy jewellery Q1 gold demand down 30%," or "Turkish gold jewellery demand seen falling 20%."

Given the sentiment in the market, it has been extremely easy for traders to shrug off these stories—a classic case of ignoring bad news. However, they have generally been able to take comfort from the inflow of gold into the various ETFs.

While analysts may try to follow the large number of these gold pools around the world, traders only really care about SPDR Gold

Shares (previously called streetTRACKS), unless someone prods them to point out a big move in Johannesburg or wherever. Even then, since the flows only come out after the markets have closed, it is seen more as an indicator of investor sentiment.

However, where it is key is in accounting for physical offtake. The traditional markets may suffer in the high price environment—indeed even seeing scrap selling rather than just declining buying—but as long as the decline in this market is offset by the interest in the ETFs, gold can be propelled to new highs, even without the assistance of one of its traditional mainstays. In other words, investment demand replaces physical demand.

·≈[Miners]≈·

Gold producers are still clearly sellers of gold. It is just that they have changed their methodology. In the past the banks' commodity trading desks were mainly set up to service the needs of this sector, which, in many instances, involved selling production from future years.

Demands from the miners' shareholders have almost totally ended this as an activity. This in turn has improved sentiment, which has obviated the need for forward selling to a large extent anyway. Indeed, probably the main business that the banks are competing with each other is to provide the producers with assistance, or clever structures, in unwinding the existing hedges. This move has been so pronounced that companies who were a key component of global supply became an important element of demand for a while. With almost all of the hedge books now unwound most of their business now involves selling their annual production, often just on a spot basis and at its most basic on a daily basis.

·≈[The Reality of Central Banks and Gold]≈·

I mentioned central banks under the section on gold as a quasi commodity, particularly in reference to their role as potential buyers. But perhaps the fact that they are perceived as buyers is rather closer to the truth.

The record of central banks in the gold market has been over-whelmingly that of sellers. While the buyers are China (although it is not clear when), Argentina, Poland, and some minimal peripheral interest in certain countries where there is a domestic mining industry (such as the Philippines), the list of sellers is far longer. The United Kingdom, Australia, Switzerland, France, Belgium, Austria, the United Arab Emirates, Sweden, Canada, and Portugal have all been sellers of gold. And this is not an exhaustive list.

Admittedly this is a fairly Euro-centric list of institutions, but they are also the nations with generally the largest gold holdings and largest percentage of metal in their reserves. During the 1990s the central banks were uniformly seen as sellers as a bloc, particularly after Australia, Switzerland, and the U.K. had all announced selling plans. However, the European central bank Gold Agreement took this uncertainty away and was successful to such an extent that this activity is no longer regarded as an overhang. Indeed the market views 500 tonnes of selling per annum (per quota year in fact) as being contained in the gold price and is more interested if there are shortfalls to this number, i.e., if that number is not reached then it is seen as a bullish signal.

The other factor where central banks influence the gold price is via interest rate policy.

·≍[Inflation]≍·

As a whole, low interest rate environments are positive for gold, and indeed for almost all investments. The logic is simple. If there is a 10-percent interest rate and gold is trading at $1,000 then gold needs to move up a *guaranteed* $100 over the course of a year to yield as much as the risk-free alternative—placing money on deposit or in T-bills, etc. Clearly no free market can offer a guaranteed return and thus the antic-ipation has to be for a much greater move. Alternatively, if the interest rate is merely 1 percent then an investment becomes more compelling and particularly if real interest rates are negative.

However, with global economic growth and inflation contained, the central bankers were clearly doing an excellent job. Inflation was not seen as a threat as the monetary authorities would simply raise rates to contain the problem and ensure that there was little disruption to the economic nirvana. This is the point where the picture diverges sharply from gold's previous nominal high where inflation had been rampant.

That was until August 2007, the point at which "credit crunch" and "subprime crisis" entered the everyday lexicon. While Mervyn King, governor of the Bank of England, initially talked about the "moral hazard" of bailing out institutions whose own policies had been responsible for the difficulties in which they now found themselves, there was little such hesitation elsewhere, with "Ben Bernanke's helicopter" becoming a popular image—cue cartoons of the chairman of the Federal Reserve dropping huge piles of cash on a grateful population.

This divergence was also a result of the different mandates in various countries. Some central banks are charged with the well-being of the economy as a whole, while for others their task is simply to keep inflation under control. For the former group the situation seemed reasonably clear, it was a trade-off between recession and inflation. The policy was to reduce rates rapidly to stave off a crash in the housing market and to try to avert the knock-on effects, these being seen as far more immediately damaging to the country than inflation. Countries in the latter group were rather more hamstrung, and instead the various governments looked at other policies to keep the economy afloat.

Whatever the rationale though, it looked to many as though the monetary authorities were no longer omnipotent. Indeed they were as much caught up in events that they had little or no control over as the rest of us.

The result of this turmoil was twofold. First, inflation became a real concern in the major Western economies, and most importantly in the U.S., for many years. Second, there was much less trust in the system and the ability of the authorities to control events.

This environment leads to the last part of the reasons for gold's rise.

·§[Trust Me—I'm a Banker!]§·

In India roughly two-thirds of the gold that is bought is by the rural, rather than urban, economy. The inference must be that it is unlikely that the country's rich elite live in these villages and thus the gold is bought as a form of savings, in particular because the community is uncertain about the security of leaving money in banks either through lack of education or because some institutions have indeed lost their depositors' money or are seen as untrustworthy.

With the major financial centers seemingly blessed by strong regulation and well-run institutions, the lure of gold in developed countries could be seen as considerably diminished. However, the recent slew of headlines in the press regarding the enormous write downs that a large number of banks have had to make, and most dramatically the sale to JP MorganChase of Bear Stearns, jolted some out of their complacency: although, for many this was a sign that the authorities were determined to ensure the stability of the financial system and to protect it over the long term.

Whatever the rationale there is no doubt that faith in the global financial system was damaged. Not only for the general population but within the industry itself; the credit crunch being made worse by banks being unwilling to lend to each other as they were simply not confident in the financial well-being of the borrowers. So when in doubt keep your cash on hand.

The other aspect about gold is that it is reassuringly simple. In a situation where banks are accused of "marking to myth" rather than "marking to market," an investment whose value is readily checkable (and saleable) is something of a comfort. Indeed, some of the early motivation behind commodity investments was the simplicity of the story, supply bottlenecks and growing demand from China et al. And it is a story that can easily be understood without an inordinate number of assumptions. Gold clearly benefited from this desire for simplicity in the early days of its rally, and this trend accelerated once the scale of the problems in financial systems became clear. Or perhaps a truer description might be that since much of the press comment has been for calls of more clarity, it was uncertainty elsewhere that saw gold breach $1,000.

In such a situation it is comforting to have an investment that is not anyone else's obligation. In other words, this was an environment tailor made to boost interest in gold.

Conclusion

So it was not any one feature that took gold to its all-time highs. Instead it was a number of issues that came together to propel the market higher. While the importance of these various factors will fluctuate, there is little doubt that the current economic and investing environment has rekindled interest in gold for many reasons, something that is unlikely to change suddenly.

Getting Exposure to Gold

 Hopefully you are now armed with enough information to try and interpret what is going on in the gold market; whether traders are slavishly following the fortunes of the U.S. dollar, or perhaps gold is moving without regard to other markets (how the metal is faring against the euro). Is it a wider commodities rally? Is gold acting as a diversifier? What is going on in the global economy? Have there been any pronouncements recently from central banks or sovereign wealth funds?

Nevertheless, the most important factor is going to be sentiment. Can the market shrug off bad news? Clearly doing the homework by asking questions like these is always going to be crucial, but even more so if the position is an outright long trade rather than using gold as a portfolio diversifier. In the latter case, the general assumption is that just about any time is going to make sense.

Before running through the various alternatives, I have to admit that I am not a financial advisor. I deal with large financial institutions that operate complex risk evaluation systems and which are required to undergo all sorts of checks before I am even allowed to talk to them. The rationale for any trade is might be completely different for small companies and private individuals where the motivation, and risk appetite, could be based on totally divergent criteria; in which case it obviously makes sense to consult a financial advisor who clearly understands the relevant needs and potential risks before entering into any such trades.

Equities

If you are convinced that it is appropriate to take a position in gold, then how should you go about it? Via physical, futures ETFs, or mining shares? Personally I know nothing about equities so I am not going to even bother to try to explain them. However, if you buy a junior explorer that discovers some enormous untapped seam, then it would seem likely that you are going to end up by making far more money than if you were simply long of gold. The problem is finding this miracle stock. Alternatively, you might be long via one of the large mining companies as a closer proxy to the gold price; but then what is going to make this company outperform, and what happens if the gold price rallies because this mining company has had to shut a mine because of safety concerns? Potentially you have the right position—gold rallies; but in the wrong place as your shares go down. All of this seems to be rather complicated to me unless you know the sector extremely well.

Physical

There is always the direct route. If you are bullish for gold then what could be more practical than actually owning a lump of it? Should the global economy start to fall apart you have the ultimate insurance, an investment outside of the usual financial world, assuming that you keep your investment somewhere safe. If you had kept a safe deposit box at Northern Rock (a British savings institution that experienced a run on it during 2007), then you would have been lining up outside with everyone else desperate to ensure that your "money" was safe. Of course you could open an account with a "too big to fail" institution (if there is such a thing), but it does somewhat take away from the rationale that sparked the decision to buy and particularly the decision to buy physical. Instead, then, do you keep it at home? Do you buy a safe to store it in? What about general security? What happens if you get robbed?

These questions do not even take into consideration such concerns as the tax regime of where you live. Is there a goods and services tax payable? Is it reclaimable once you sell it? Perhaps even more importantly, what is the markup? How much is the retailer going to charge you over the loco London price? Obviously you are not going to march into Tiffany's to buy a chain with five ounces of gold in it, but what is the premium that you are paying and are you better off buying Canadian maples, Australian nuggets, Chinese pandas, Austrian philharmonikers, or any of the plethora of other bullion gold coins that exist? Is it worth considering gold coins that have a numismatic value? Probably not, if you want exposure to the gold price rather than introducing additional variables such as provenance, condition, and so on.

Or is perhaps buying a few small bars a better idea? It is worth noting that as a general rule, the smaller the bar or coin, the greater the premium that you will end up paying.

⊶[Futures]⊷

If you are not concerned that the world financial system is in imminent danger of folding, then you may well be better off by getting exposure to gold via futures, unallocated gold, or ETFs. If your rationale is to take a simple short-term trading position, then, depending on the size of investment, you could well be better off by trading in the futures markets. Most likely in your own currency, but if not, then most people would probably look to the U.S. market and particularly the CME Globex® electronic trading system. These venues allow for quick movements in and out of positions anonymously, but they may be more of a problem for larger investors or traders as the liquidity is often better in OTC markets than in the futures.

However, if, rather than trading gold, the motive is for a long-term holding, and perhaps diversification, then futures are a rather more cumbersome way of expressing this view. Which contract month do you want to go long of? Each time the month becomes due, the position then needs to be rolled into the next active period, and so on—not disastrous, but just a little inconvenient.

⊶❘ Unallocated Gold ❘⊷

As for having an unallocated account with a bank, this is a simple way of trading in gold; in fact it is very similar to any other account that you might hold with them. Statements will arrive showing your particular balance; a simple phone call to the institution will allow you to add to this or indeed to reduce it—all very neat. However, the problem is that normally trading rooms are set up to deal with large institutions such as other banks, hedge funds, sovereign wealth funds, central banks, pension funds, and the like. They also tend to impose rules regarding the minimum sizes of trades, perhaps 1,000 ounces of gold and 50,000 ounces of silver. They also may not have time to discuss the vagaries of the prevailing market, unless you are a very large-volume customer. Indeed, in many jurisdictions, staff in trading rooms are forbidden by law to talk to private individuals and can only converse with other market professionals; this rule is to ensure that the general public are served by people who have a better understanding of their risk profile.

Indeed, a conversation on gold I might have with a hedge fund, at its briefest, might simply be:

Hedge Fund: Gold in 20k.

Banker: 20–70.

Hedge Fund: At 70.

Banker: Done.

The entire process lasts little more than 15 seconds.

The translation of this conversation is:

Hedge Fund: Gold in 20,000 ounces, please.

Banker: I would buy at $975.20 and sell at $975.70.

Hedge Fund: I buy 20,000 ounces.

Banker: Agreed, we sell you 20,000 ounces of gold at $ 975.70.

So ultimately it is very likely that the private individual will end up by dealing through their private banker or local branch, and even then, the business might not meet the minimum size requirements.

In effect, trading directly with the various bullion banks is an option only open to large institutions or professional investors.

ETFs

There is also the case for ETFs, which are essentially just shares. If an investor is looking to buy gold for diversification, then clearly there is a portfolio that needs to be diversified. Obviously it is likely to contain at least some equities, and therefore the individual is likely to already have a relationship with a stockbroker or someone in a similar position. In which case, the ETF can simply be added via this route. Because the ETF is effectively only one-tenth of an ounce of gold, then it can accommodate small purchases, and there is easy freedom of movement, with no concerns over security, goods and services taxes, and so on. Also, since it is relatively easy for trading houses to arbitrage between loco London and the ETF, it is likely to always track the gold price closely. Therefore, it seems that the only real issues for the investor are the charges levied and whether the company backing the scheme is creditworthy.

A romantic notion of the ETF would be that each investor would own a percentage of a specific gold bar, directly. So that in theory you could have marched in to the custodian and demanded to see that bar. In practice they would never have allowed you to do this, of course, because banks generally do not like the general public knowing where large quantities of gold are stored, let alone taking them on guided tours; although the Federal Reserve Bank of New York is an honorable exception that does indeed allow visitors to their vaults; for details, see its Web site (www.newyorkfed.org).

Anyway, the actual problem with this was the impossible logistics; you might want to sell your portion of a gold bar, but what about the other people who own the other bits of the bar? Therefore, instead of owning the gold itself, you end up owning shares in a trust whose only asset is gold. Not quite the same thing for many people, but the ETFs have been an astounding success and have created a whole new class of investors.

·⊰[Structured Notes]⊱·

For investors who require a different type of product but still want exposure to the gold price, there are various structured notes for them to invest in. The following two ideas are from Barclays Capital Commodity Investor Solutions, as much as anything just to give an idea of the types of trades that investors have been looking at. Obviously, as with all pricing in this book, the levels are indicative and purely for illustration; in neither of the two examples that follow does the investor actually own gold, but instead the investor is exposed to a structure where the return is based on the performance of gold.

Both of these types of structured notes are capital guaranteed, so in return for no downside, should the gold price move lower, there is no conventional full participation in the upside. However, because the second structure has a floating strike call, it is possible to benefit even if gold is at the same price, or even if it is lower, at the end of two years as it was at the start.

The first structure is a two-year note with 28 percent participation on a gold rally. If at maturity gold is up by 40 percent, the client receives 40 percent × 28 percent, or 11.5 percent. If gold is down at maturity, there is no payoff, but no capital is lost. Obviously, it is simple to understand and to see the trade-off between no loss if gold goes lower but only limited participation as it rallies.

The second, rather more esoteric structure rejoices under the name of the floating shark fin note. It is called a shark fin because the call option can knock out if gold ever increases by 45 percent of its initial price (continuous observation). In other words, yield can go up steeply but plummet if gold rallies 45 percent from its starting price, then the final return would be zero, although the principal would still be protected.

As above, the call is a floating strike being determined as the lowest price observed during the two-year period of the note according to a specified strike schedule. For example, if gold ever trades below $900, it will be $900; and if it ever trades below $850, the strike is $850; if it ever trades below $800, the strike is $800; and so on.

If at maturity gold is up by 40 percent from the set strike, then the investor receives a 40 percent return (compared to 11.5 percent with the standard bull note above). Even if gold has fallen over the period, then it is still possible to make money as the strike will be lower.

For example: On the trade date gold is $935 per ounce. At some point during the two years it falls below $800 (and the floating strike call is set there). Then, at maturity gold is trading at $900. The investor would make ((900/800) − 1) percent = 12.5 percent. Under the standard bull note the yield would be zero.

However—and this is a big however—should gold rally and ever trade, during the two-year duration of this structure above $1,350 (in this example), then the investor would simply receive their principal back at maturity.

Conclusion

The environment for gold has changed enormously over the last few years. The resurgence of inflation as a potential threat, the lessening of confidence in the financial system as both banks and the monetary authorities have shown themselves struggling to contain events, the weaker dollar, and the emergence of gold and commodities as a reinvigorated asset class have all added to the positive sentiment that surrounds gold.

Should the investor (and the investor's advisors) decide that gold suits their portfolio, then there are a great number of ways in which to take advantage of this. The course of action will depend on risk profile and circumstances, but the investment could be via physical gold, some form of gold-backed note, or simply, and perhaps most suitably, in my view, via the ETF.

However, whatever the ultimate route it seems unlikely that gold will relinquish the opportunity to once again be a significant feature in global financial markets.

"Rules" for Trading Gold

 Obviously these rules are nothing more than personal opinion and are just a short checklist to bear in mind. The final point is somewhat tongue in cheek!

1. What is your motivation—diversification or appreciation?

2. What time frame are you considering holding gold for?

3. What is your view of the U.S. dollar?

4. How has gold performed against the euro?

5. What is the geopolitical picture?

6. What is market sentiment?

7. How much attention is gold receiving?

8. Have central banks or sovereign wealth funds announced plans?

9. Take a look at the charts.

10. Never trust silver!

Silver trades very differently from gold and is generally far more volatile. It has even fewer fundamentals of its own than gold, some 70 percent of its production is a by-product of mining other metals. Silver also tends to attract highly speculative money that wants to get involved in precious metals but considers gold to be too expensive.

Nevertheless trading the gold/silver ratio is quite a common practice. Generally silver will move more dramatically than gold; so it can work to buy silver and sell gold (in a bullish environment for gold), i.e., sell the ratio, and do the opposite where gold is considered to be in a bear market. However, much effectiveness of this trade will depend on the relative level of the prices at inception.

FAQs

1. How much gold has ever been mined?

   By the end of 2007 total mined gold had reached 161,000 tonnes. (Data from GFMS: Gold Survey 2008.)

2. Which country produces the most gold?

   In 2007 it was China with 280.5 tonnes, followed by South Africa at 269.9, and Australia at 246.3 tonnes. The United States was fourth with 239.5 tonnes. (Data from GFMS: Gold Survey 2008.)

3. Which is the world's largest gold mining company?

   Barrick Gold, which produced 250.7 tonnes in 2007.

4. How much gold is mined each year?

   2,476 tonnes of gold were mined globally in 2007, whereas in 2000 that figure was 2,618. (Data from GFMS: Gold Survey 2008.)

5. What is the production cost for gold?

   Total production costs rose 25 percent in 2007 to $496 with cash costs of $395 per ounce. (Data from GFMS: Gold Survey 2008.)

6. What is the world's deepest gold mine?

   Gold Fields Driefontein Mine at 4,121 meters (a little over two and one-half miles) deep. (Data from Virtual Metals Group.)

7. What is the world's most productive mine?

   It is Newmont's Nevada Mine, which produced 72.81 tonnes of gold in 2007. That was down from 2006's level when it produced nearly 79 tonnes, but in 2006 it was Yanacocha in Peru (also operated by Newmont) that took the crown with 81.247 tonnes. (Data from Virtual Metals Group.)

8. Which country consumes the most gold?

   India consumed 555.1 tonnes of gold jewelry in 2007, with China in second place at 302.2 tonnes. (Data from GFMS: Gold Survey 2008.)

9. What is the biggest use of gold?

   Jewelry consumption—in 2007 it was 2,401 tonnes down from 3,204 tonnes in 2000. (Data from GFMS: Gold Survey 2008).

10. What is "Identifiable Investment" for gold?

    In 2007 this reached 654 tonnes, up from 165 tonnes in 2000. (Data from GFMS: Gold Survey 2008.)

11. What is the supply/demand balance?

    In 2007 it was 3,912 tonnes, down from 4,017 tonnes in 2000. Supply, apart from mine supply, is from official sector sales (481 tonnes) and gold scrap (956 tonnes). (Data from GFMS: Gold Survey 2008.)

12. How much gold do central banks hold?

    Some 29,700 or so tonnes. It is difficult to get exact figures as it is claimed that there is both under- and overreporting in the IMF statistics. Additionally balances will change as the central banks buy and sell gold.

13. Which country holds the most gold?

    The United States has the world's largest gold reserves, holding 8,133.50 tons. At a price of $970 this amount would be worth in excess of $252 billion. However, if the United States decided it was going to sell its gold then the price would be significantly lower—very quickly!

14. Where do central banks hold their gold?

    The vast majority of central banks hold their gold in allocated form. Some might be held in their own vaults, some might be in the Federal Reserve Bank in New York. However, any central bank that wants to trade its gold must hold it in the Bank of England (if in allocated form), because the Bank of England's vaults are in London and metal held there can be easily moved in and out of the clearing system.

    However, it is extremely easy to defer delivery and allow time to ship the gold. In certain transactions a central bank might lend gold loco the Federal Reserve Bank in New York and receive it back at the Bank of England in London. Or simply sell it loco New York; leaving the bullion bank to make the shipping arrangements.

15. What is the WGC?

    "Founded in 1987, the World Gold Council is an organization formed and funded by the world's leading gold mining companies with the aim of stimulating and maximizing the demand for, and holding of, gold by consumers, investors, industry, and the official sector.

    As well as undertaking marketing initiatives to drive demand, the World Gold Council is also instrumental in working to lower regulatory barriers to the widespread ownership of gold products, helping to develop distribution systems, and promoting the role of gold as a reserve asset in the official sector." Their Web site is www.gold.org.

16. What is GFMS?

According to the GFMS Web site, "GFMS is the world's foremost precious metals consultancy, specializing in research into the global gold, silver, platinum and palladium markets. GFMS is based in London, U.K., but has representation in Australia, India, China, Germany, France, Spain and Russia, and a vast range of contacts and associates across the world. Our research team of fifteen full-time analysts comprises qualified and experienced economists and geologists; while two consultants contribute insights on important regional markets." Their Web site is www.gfms.co.uk.

17. What is Virtual Metals?

"Established in 1997 and expanded in 2001, the VM Group is an independent commodities research consultancy covering precious and base metals, energy, and agricommodities. VMG specializes in macro-economic analysis of these commodities, both of the fundamentals, through generation of supply and demand scenarios, and in-depth understanding of related investment and derivatives markets. Using this analysis we derive for our clients price forecasts, projections concerning future supply/demand, and strategic recommendations.

Through VMG's collaboration with Fortis Bank, the company offers a full range of independent and comprehensive publications in commodity markets that are available on a complementary basis." For more information contact info@vmgroup.co.uk.

18. What is the LBMA?

"The LBMA is the trade association that acts as the co-ordinator for activities conducted on behalf of its members and other participants in the London bullion market. It acts as the principal point of contact between the market and its regulators. Through its staff and its committees, it works to ensure that London continues to meet the evolving needs of the global bullion market." The LBMA Web site is www.lbma.org.uk.

19. Does gold have an interest rate?

Contrary to many people's expectations it does. However, there is no central authority looking to set rates, instead it is simply a question of supply and demand. Traditionally the vast majority of supply has been from central banks and the demand from gold mining companies for hedging purposes. In the almost total absence of hedging, gold interest rates have sunk and the metal yields very little; only around 10 basis points (0.10 percent) for one month and just 60 basis points (0.6 percent) for 10 years on a semiannual basis.

20. What is GOFO?

GOFO is a corruption of GOld FOrward and is the Reuters page where gold lending rates, on a swap basis, are published every day.

21. What does the price of gold in the newspaper mean?

Obviously it will vary from country to country but if it is in dollars and does not give a month indication next to it, then it is likely to be the spot price for a troy ounce of loco London unallocated gold.

22. What is the "standard" price for gold?

The loco London spot price is the standard. Gold to be delivered in any other location or purity or bar size will be quoted as a premium or discount to this price.

23. Is there a benchmark price for gold?

The London gold fixing is universally accepted as the benchmark price. This takes place twice each day at 10.30 a.m. and 3 p.m. London time. From time to time there is a debate about whether either of these two fixings is more representative than the other. In my opinion each are equally valid, although it is occasionally argued that the afternoon fixing is more important as it takes place when both London and New York are open for business.

24. What does loco London mean?

Gold settles over accounts in London in the same way that U.S. dollars do in New York or Japanese yen in Tokyo. As such gold is loco London, and dollars are loco New York and yen loco Tokyo although the terminology isn't used in these markets.

25. What is a loco swap?

A loco swap is an agreement to exchange equivalent quantities of gold in two separate locations. One location will almost invariably be London but the other could be a variety of places such as Zurich, Germiston (at the Rand Refinery just outside Johannesburg, South Africa), the Federal Reserve in New York, and so on.

The trade is booked as the purchase of gold in one location and the sale of an equivalent amount in the other. The price differential will be a reflection of the demand for gold in each location but at its simplest may be nothing more than the cost of shipping the metal in to London, plus refining costs if necessary.

26. What is a troy ounce?

The troy ounce is the standard unit of measurement for gold. In everyday life we use avoirdupois ounces, which are smaller than troy ounces, or ounces troy as is the correct terminology but which is almost never used. The term troy is thought to originate from a medieval gold fair that was held in the French town of Troies. A troy ounce is 1.09714 standard ounces.

27. What is a London Good Delivery bar?

The London Bullion Market association sets the definitions as "The physical settlement of a loco London gold trade is a bar conforming to the following specifications:

- *Weight: Minimum gold content: 350 fine troy ounces (approximately 10.9 kilograms)*

- *Maximum gold content: 430 fine troy ounces (approximately 13.4 kilograms).*

> *The gross weight of a bar should be expressed in troy ounces, in multiples of 0.025, rounded down to the nearest 0.025 of a troy ounce.*

> *Dimensions: The recommended dimensions for a Good Delivery gold bar are approximately as follows:*

> *Length (Top): 250 mm +/− 40 mm Undercut: 7 percent to 15 percent*

> *Width (Top): 70 mm +/− 15 mm Undercut: 15 percent to 30 percent*

> *Height: 35 mm +/− 10 mm*

> *The undercut refers to the degree of slope on the side and ends of the bar and is calculated by deducting the dimension of the bottom edge of the bar from the dimension of the top edge and dividing the result by the top edge dimension multiplied by one hundred to obtain the percentage undercut.*

> *Fineness: The minimum acceptable fineness is 995.0 parts per thousand fine gold." Additionally, each bar has to have a serial number, the stamp of the refiner, year of manufacture, and fineness of gold to four significant figures.*

28. What is contango?

The gold market is almost invariably "in contango." This means that the forward price—the price for delivery of gold further ahead than two business days—is higher than the spot price. This gap is to account for the relative differences in gold and U.S. dollar interest rates with the latter normally higher than the former.

29. What is backwardation?

For more traditional commodities they have generally tended to be in backwardation—the exact reverse of contango—to reflect their relative scarcity and the need of companies to use them in manufacturing, etc. So that the prices "further down the curve,"

*which means for delivery at a later date, are lower than those
for immediate delivery.*

30. What are the main trading centers for gold?

    *For Asia they are Sydney, Singapore, Hong Kong, and Tokyo.
    For Europe they are London and Zurich. For the Americas it is
    New York.*

31. How many market makers are there in gold?

    *It depends on who you are and what you do. However, in each
    trading center there are no more than 11 interbank market
    makers, institutions that are obligated to make two-way prices
    to each other. However, there will be many other institutions
    that will make markets to their customers.*

32. Which group is the most influential in the gold market?

    *Without a doubt it used to be the gold mining companies via
    their hedging programs, and then when they unwound their
    hedge books. However, it is probably now the hedge funds, both
    when gold was a version of the "carry trade" and more recently
    when gold has been a favored tool to express an economic view.
    Central banks are also clearly important, when announcing a
    sale or purchase, but generally their influence does not impact
    the gold market on a day-to-day basis. Indeed all the central
    banks that I have ever talked to on gold (probably some 60 or so)
    do not want to impact the market in any way.*

33. What are allocated and unallocated gold?

    *If you hold allocated gold on account then you know exactly
    which bars you own. Indeed your statement will list each bar,
    its gross weight, fineness (purity), and net weight. If you have
    an unallocated account then it will simply list the amount of
    gold that you own.*

    *My favorite analogy is the difference between having a safe
    deposit box and a checking account. In the same way that the
    majority of us have checking accounts rather than safe deposit*

boxes the same is true for participants in the gold market; unallocated gold is the more typical form of ownership.

34. Is the gold market regulated?

    This will vary by jurisdiction, but as a general guide trading on exchange or by other form of derivative is more likely to be subject to regulation in a particular country. In the United Kingdom, for example, it is the Financial Services Authority that has responsibility for regulated activities. In the United States, the New York Mercantile Exchange is regulated by the Commodity Futures Trading Commission (CFTC) and exchange-traded notes are traded on exchanges such as the New York Stock Exchange (NYSE), which are regulated by the Securities and Exchange Commission (SEC).

35. What is the EcbGA?

    It stands for European central bank Gold Agreement. The bizarre mixture of upper and lower case letters is supposed to represent that it is an agreement by European central banks rather than by the European Central Bank (the Frankfurt-based institution that is the main central bank for countries who have the euro as their currency and is responsible for setting interest rates among other things). The original agreement was signed on September 26, 1999 and ran for five years over which its 15 signatories limited themselves to selling 2,000 tonnes of gold and no more than 400 tonnes in any quota year (which begins on September 27 and continues through the following September 26). The follow-up, also for five years, increased the amount to 2,500 tonnes and no more than 500 in any quota year.

36. Is there a conspiracy to manipulate the gold price?

    I have worked at four banks—Credit Suisse, Chase Manhattan, Deutsche Bank, and Barclays Bank—these are some of the world's most important "bullion banks," and all were market makers when I worked for them. In my 25 years I have never seen evidence of any conspiracy, and indeed the overwhelming attitude of central banks has been to take a low profile within the market. For the avoidance of doubt, I have never met anyone working in the precious metals division of a major bank who believes in such conspiracy theories.

37. What is GATA?

GATA notes that "[The] Gold Anti-Trust Action Committee was organized in January 1999 to advocate and undertake litigation against illegal collusion to control the price and supply of gold and related financial securities." Their Web site is www.gata.org.

38. What is No Dirty Gold?

No Dirty Gold describes itself as not seeking to boycott gold or metals but as an effort to "promote responsible mining practices and phase out irresponsible practices ... Thus far, more than 30 major jewellery retailers have endorsed the No Dirty Gold campaign's criteria for more responsible mining—also known as 'The Golden Rules.' These retailers, including such major corporations as Signet in the UK, Tiffany & Co. and Wal-Mart in the United States, and Cartier/Richemont in Europe, have also committed to sourcing gold and precious metals from operations that meet these social and environmental criteria. In 2006, a multi-stakeholder initiative (including NGOs like Earthworks and Oxfam America, jewellery retailers, mining companies, labour unions, and mining-affected communities) called IRMA was launched, with the objective of developing a system for independent verification of compliance with environmental and social standards for mining operations. No Dirty Gold has also helped to spur the development of CRJP, the Council for Responsible Jewellery Practices (an association of mining and jewellery companies promoting greater corporate responsibility among its members)." For more information see: http://www.nodirtygold.org/supporting_retailers.cfm, http://www.responsiblemining.net/, and http://www.responsiblejewellery.com/.

FAQs

39. What is ARM?

ARM calls itself "an independent, global-scale effort, and pioneer initiative, created as an international and multi-institutional organisation to bring credibility, transparency and legitimacy to the development of a framework for responsible artisanal and small-scale mining." It further is looking to consumers to change their habits by educating "consumers as to their power to directly improve the quality of life of artisanal miners by purchasing fair trade jewellery and minerals." The ARM Web site is www.communitymining.org.

Glossary of Terms

(This glossary is provided courtesy of the London Bullion Market Association and the London Platinum and Palladium Market.)

Accelerated Supply   Precious metal sold to the market before it is physically produced—generally created by producer hedging or finance transactions.

Aliquot   A small representative sample taken from a precious metals bar for assay to determine its fine precious metals content.

Allocated Accounts   These accounts are opened when a customer requires metal to be physically segregated and needs a detailed list of weights and assays.

Alloy   A mixture of two or more chemical elements, including at least one metal. In the case of gold, it is mixed with a baser metal or metals to lower the purity, influence the color, or add durability.

American-Style Option   An option, which can be exercised at any stage during its life, at or before expiration date.

Arbitrage   Simultaneous buying and selling of the same asset in different markets in order to capitalize on variations in price between those markets.

Asian-Style Option   An option that, if it expires in-the-money, is automatically settled on the basis of the difference between the strike price and the average price of the underlying asset in a given period prior to expiration.

Ask   The price a dealer or seller asks for a commodity.

Assay   The determination of the precious metal content of an alloy, either using a direct method (where the actual precious metal content is measured) or an indirect, instrumental method (usually based on spectrographic analysis) in which the levels of impurities are measured and the precious metal content is calculated by difference. For gold, the main direct method is fire assay, also known as cupellation or gravimetric analysis.

Assayer   A tester of precious metals.

Assay Mark   The stamp by an assayer on a bar or piece of precious metal to guarantee its fineness.

Assay Office   An official or statutory organization controlling the testing of precious metals within a country.

At the Money   Refers to an option strike price that is equal to the current market price of the underlying asset.

Australian Securities Exchange   The ASX was formed in 2006 following the merger of the Sydney Futures Exchange with the Australian Stock Exchange. Web site: www.asx.com.au

Average Strike Options   Asian-style options where the ultimate settlement depends on an average strike price rather than an average underlying asset price.

Averaging   A method whereby a smoothing of the fluctuations in price movements may be achieved by agreeing to buy or sell a specified total quantity of precious metal on the basis of average prices over an agreed period of time.

Glossary of Terms

Backwardation A market situation where prices for future delivery are lower than the spot price, caused by shortage or tightness of supply.

Bank of England Founded in 1694, "The Old Lady of Threadneedle Street" has been the focal point of gold and silver trading in London for over three centuries. It is one of the most active central banks in gold and is the gold depository for many of the world's central banks. Web site: www.bankofengland.co.uk

Bar Chart A type of chart commonly used in technical analysis that shows highs, lows, and closing prices.

Barrier Options Exotic options that either come to life (are knocked-in) or are extinguished (knocked-out) under conditions stipulated in the options contract. The conditions are usually defined in terms of a price level (barrier, knock-out, or knock-in price) that may be reached at any time during the lifetime of the option. There are four major types of barrier options: up-and-out, up-and-in, down-and-out, and down-and-in. The extinguishing or activating features of these options mean that they are usually cheaper than ordinary options, making them attractive to purchasers looking to avoid high premium.

Bear Someone who expects prices to fall.

Bear Call Spread The purchase and sale of call options at different exercise prices but with the same expiry date. The purchased (or long) calls have a higher exercise price than the written (or short) calls. The investor expects a fall in the price of the underlying asset.

Bear Market A market in which the trend is for prices to decline.

Bear Put Spread The purchase and sale of put options at different exercise prices but with the same expiry date. The puts purchased have a higher exercise price than the puts written. The investor expects a fall in the price of the underlying asset.

Bermuda-Style Option Exotic options that combine certain features of American- and European-style options. They may be exercised on predetermined dates during the lifetime of the option or on the expiry date. (See also **American-Style Option** and **European-Style Option.**)

Beta   The beta of a rate or price is the extent to which that rate or price follows movements in the overall market. If the beta is greater than one, it is more volatile than the market; if the beta is less than one, it is less volatile.

Bid   The price at which a dealer is willing to buy.

BIS   Bank for International Settlements. Based in Basel, Switzerland, it was founded in 1930 and now acts as a nonpolitical central bank for central banks. Web site: www.bis.org

Black-Scholes Model   An option-pricing model initially derived by Fischer Black and Myron Scholes in 1973 for securities options and later refined by Black in 1976 for options on futures.

Blank   A blank disc of metal with milled edges used to make a coin.

Brazilian Mercantile and Futures Exchange   The BM&F was incorporated in July 1985. Web site: www.bmf.com.br

Britannia   British gold coin first issued in 1987 with a fineness of 916.6.

Breakout/Breakaway GAP   In technical analysis, this occurs when prices break out of their trading range, leaving a gap in the chart. It is associated with an increase in volume and is regarded as a strong trend signal.

Broker   An intermediary between traders for physical, futures, and over-the-counter deals. Brokers receive a fixed commission predetermined between the broker and his/her client.

Budapest Stock Exchange   The Budapest Stock Exchange had its origins in the Hungarian Stock Exchange, which was formed in 1864. Following World War II, the Exchange was dissolved by the government and was reestablished on June 21, 1990. Commodity trading was introduced on November 2, 2005. Web site: www.bse.hu

Bull   Someone who expects prices to rise.

Bull Call Spread   The purchase and sale of call options at different exercise prices but with the same expiry date. The purchased (or long) calls have a lower price than the written (or short) calls. The investor expects a rise in the price of the underlying asset.

Bull Market   A market in which the trend is for prices to increase.

Bull Put Spread   The purchase and sale of put options at different exercise prices but with the same expiry date. The puts purchased have a lower exercise price than the puts written. The investor expects the price of the underlying asset to rise.

Bullion   The generic word for gold and silver in bar or ingot form. Originally meant "mint" or "melting place" from the old French word *bouillon,* which means boiling.

Bullion and Precious Metal Coins   Contemporary precious metal coins minted in unlimited numbers for investment purposes.

Butterfly Spread   The simultaneous purchase of an out-of-the-money **strangle** and sale of an at-the-money-**straddle**. The buyer profits if the underlying remains stable and has limited risk in the event of a large move in either direction.

Buy Signal   In technical analysis, a chart pattern that indicates a key reversal upwards in price and the time to buy.

Calendar Spread   The simultaneous purchase and sale (or vice versa) of an option of the same strike for different months.

Call Option   An option that gives the purchaser the right, but not the obligation, to buy an asset at a predetermined price on or by a set date.

Cap   An options contract whereby the seller agrees to pay to the purchaser, in return for a premium, the difference between a reference rate and an agreed strike price when the reference exceeds the strike on or before a specific date.

Carat Derived from the word for "carob" in various languages, it was originally equivalent to the weight of the seed of the carob tree. It has two meanings in modern usage: (1) a measure of the weight of precious stones: one carat = 0.2053 grams; (2) a measure of the proportion of gold in a gold alloy, on the basis that 24 carat is pure gold, often expressed as K or k, e.g., 18k is 75 percent gold.

Cash and Carry The purchase (or sale) of an underlying spot asset and the simultaneous sale (or purchase) of a futures or forward contract.

CFTC Commodity Futures Trading Commission. The U.S. government's regulatory agency for all U.S. future markets. Web site: www.cftc.gov

Chartist An analyst who forecasts future price trends by the technical interpretation of chart patterns based on historical prices.

Chervonetz A Russian bullion coin, 900 fine with fine gold content of 0.2489 troy ounces and a face value of 10 rubles, which was issued in the 1970s.

Chinese Gold and Silver Exchange Society Hong Kong's exchange first opened in 1910 and became the Chinese Gold and Silver Exchange Society in 1918. Web site: www.cgse.com.hk

Chinese Wall A barrier to the flow of information between two different parts of a firm's business.

Chop Assay mark of Chinese origin. The term is now widely applied to a manufacturer's mark on bullion bars.

CIF Cost, insurance, and freight. A CIF price includes the cost of material together with transport and insurance costs to the final specified destination.

CME Group The CME Group was formed by the 2007 merger of the Chicago Mercantile Exchange (CME) and the Chicago Board of Trade (CBOT). Web site: www.cmegroup.com

Coin Gold   A gold alloy, usually with a minimum fine gold content of 900, prepared for making coins, usually with silver or copper, to improve durability.

Collar   A supply contract between a buyer and a seller of a commodity, whereby the buyer is assured that he will not have to pay more than some maximum price, and whereby the seller is assured of receiving some minimum price.

COMEX   The Commodity Exchange in New York, a division of **NYMEX**.

Compound Options   These are options on options. The underlying asset is an option rather than a tangible commodity or security.

Consignment Stocks   These are gold or silver bars that are placed by an organization with a client against a guarantee of payment at the prevailing price as the metal is taken out of the stock.

Contango   The market situation where the price for future (forward) delivery is greater than the spot price.

Cost of Carry   The cost of holding a physical commodity over a period of time. The main elements are funding costs, storage, and insurance.

Covered Option   A covered call option is one where the writer owns the underlying asset on which the option is written. A covered put option is one where the writer sells the option while holding cash.

Day Order   An order to buy or sell at a particular price level, which is only valid for one business day.

Deferred Settlement   An arrangement whereby settlement of both sides of a bullion deal, metal and money, are deferred on a day-to-day basis.

Delivery   The actual transfer of the ownership of precious metal. It may not involve physical movement of metal and is usually made by a simple paper transfer in the clearing system.

Delivery Date   The specified day on which precious metal must be delivered to fulfill a contract.

Delta   Option risk parameter that measures the sensitivity of an option price to changes in the price of its underlying instrument.

Delta Hedging   A strategy undertaken by granters of options to protect their exposure. A delta hedge calculation takes into account changes in the spot price, the time to expiry, and the difference between the strike and spot prices.

Derivative   A financial instrument derived from a cash market commodity, futures contract, or other financial instrument. Derivatives can be traded on regulated exchange markets or over-the-counter. For example, metal futures contracts are derivatives of physical commodities; options on futures are derivatives of futures contracts.

Doré   An unrefined alloy of gold with variable quantities of silver and smaller quantities of base metals, which is produced at a mine before passing on to a refinery for upgrading to London Good Delivery standard.

Double Bottom/Double Top   In technical analysis, a double bottom occurs when the price falls to the same level twice and fails to penetrate. This signals good support. A double top is the opposite, i.e., when a price rises to the same level twice and fails to break above it, and therefore produces a level of good resistance.

Double Eagle   Gold coin with a face value of $20 issued as legal tender in the United States during the period from 1850 to 1932. It is 900 fine with a fine gold content of 0.9675 troy ounces.

Dow Theory   Developed by Charles Dow and referred to as the six tenets of Dow Theory, it addresses market psychology, price action, and marks the foundations of technical analysis. The six tenets are: 1. The averages discount everything; 2. There are three trends; 3. Major trends have three phases; 4. The averages must confirm each other; 5. Volume must confirm the trend; 6. A trend is assumed to be in effect until it gives definitive signals that it has reversed.

Dubai Gold and Commodities Exchange   The DGCX commenced trading in 2005. Web site: www.dgcx.ae

Eagle   The earliest legal tender U.S. gold coin first minted in 1795. It is 900 fine.

EFP   Exchange for Physical. Actual exchange between an OTC contract and a futures contract that takes place off exchange between parties.

Elliott Wave Theory   Developed by R.N. Elliott, the approach defines markets as moving in a predetermined number of waves. Markets move in a sequence of five waves in the direction of the underlying trend and correct in a sequence of three waves. The trend movement or impulse is labeled 1–2–3–4–5 and a correction is labeled A-B-C.

ETF/ETC   Exchange-Traded Commodities (or Exchange-Traded Funds) are open-ended, listed securities that are arbitrageable with the underlying markets. ETCs trade on stock exchanges and have multiple market makers. ETCs are either backed by the physical commodity where possible (e.g., gold, silver, platinum, palladium) or are priced off commodity futures markets, thereby providing retail and institutional equity investors with the opportunity to gain exposure to major commodities through existing equity accounts.

European-Style Option   An option that can only be exercised on the expiry date.

Exchange-Traded Options   Options on future contracts offered by a recognized futures exchange, such as NYMEX.

Exercise   The exercise by an option holder of his right to buy (call) or sell (put) an asset at the agreed strike price.

Exotic Options   The generic term for the more sophisticated option strategies that have features over and above basic option contracts.

Expiry Date   The last date on which an option can be exercised.

FAS 133   See **Financial Accounting Standards Board Statement 133**.

FCM   Futures Commission Merchant. The legal term for a U.S. commodity brokerage house handling futures exchange business.

Fibonacci Numbers   The Fibonacci sequence is calculated by adding any number in the series to the previous number: (1,2,3,5,8, 13,21,34,55,89, …). The ratio of any number in the series to the next is 0.618 and to the number two positions away, 0.382. The mid-point between 0.382 and 0.618 is 0.50. These ratios (usually shown as percentages) are known as the Fibonacci ratios and are used in technical analysis to calculate retracement levels during a correction. The inverse of 0.618 (1.618) is used in calculating (Elliott Wave) projections. Fibonacci ratios form an integral part of **Elliott Wave Theory.**

Financial Accounting Standards Board (FASB)   The private sector organization responsible for establishing standards of accounting and financial reporting in the United States.

Financial Accounting Standards Board Statement 133 (FAS 133)
FAS 133 obliges U.S. companies to put all financial derivative instruments that are not used to hedge exposure on the balance sheet at market value. Companies therefore disclose unrealized gains and losses on derivatives, rather than accounting for them only at maturity.

Fineness   The proportion of precious metal in an alloy expressed as parts in 1,000.

Fine Weight   The weight of gold contained in a bar, coin, or bullion as determined by multiplying the gross weight by the fineness.

Fire Assay   A method of determining the content of a metal (most commonly gold) in an alloy involving the removal of other metals by what is in effect a combination of fire refining (for the removal of base metals) and chemical refining (for the removal of silver) and then determining the gold content by comparing the initial and final weights of the sample. Fire assay can determine the gold content of Good Delivery–type alloys to an accuracy of better than 1 part in 10,000. Fire assay is also known as cupellation or gravimetric analysis.

Flag   In technical analysis, one of the basic chart patterns. In a bull market a flag occurs when prices consolidate for a period then continue to rise. In a bear market the converse occurs, i.e., prices resume falling after a period of consolidation.

Flat Rate Forwards   Forward contracts offering a constant contango throughout the life of the contract.

Floor   A supply contract between a buyer and seller of a commodity, whereby the seller is assured that he will receive at least some minimum price. This type of contract is analogous to a put option, which gives the holder the right to sell the underlying at a predetermined price.

FOB   Free on Board. A FOB price usually includes cost of transport, insurance, and loading onto a vessel at the port of departure.

Fool's Gold   Pyrites of iron sulphide, which is gold-like in appearance and can delude amateur prospectors.

Forward Premium   The difference between spot and forward quotations that will be determined by money and precious metal interest rates and storage charges.

Forward Transaction   Purchase or sale for delivery and payment at an agreed date in the future.

FSA   Financial Services Authority. The single financial services regulator in the United Kingdom. Web site: www.fsa.gov.uk

FSMA   The Financial Services and Markets Act 2000 is the legislation that set up the Financial Services Authority and defines its powers. It came into force in late 2001.

Fundamental Analysis   The study of basic underlying factors that will affect the supply and demand of a traded commodity.

Futures Contract   An agreement made on an organized exchange to buy or sell a specific commodity or financial instrument on a set date in the future at a set price. In practice, most futures positions are "squared off" before maturity with delivery, if it takes place, in the form of a warehouse receipt.

Gamma   The sensitivity of an option's delta to changes in the price of the underlying instrument.

Gearing   The potential to magnify profits or losses by incurring exposure to large positions from an initially small investment outlay. Also known as **Leverage**.

GOFO   Gold Forward Offered Rate. The gold equivalent to LIBOR. The rates at which dealers will lend gold on swap against U.S. dollars.

GOFRA   Gold Forward Rate Agreement. An "off balance sheet" instrument used to minimize forward gold interest rate exposure. It hedges the combined effect of moves in both U.S. dollar and gold interest rates with settlement in dollars.

Gold   Latin name *Aurum*. Chemical symbol Au. Its specific gravity is 19.32 and melting point is 1,063 degrees centigrade.

Gold Accumulation Plans (GAPs)   Gold investment accounts whereby the investor agrees to invest a certain sum of currency in gold each month. Gold accumulated in the account can later be sold back or withdrawn as physical metal in a variety of forms, including bars, coins, or jewelry.

Gold Fixing   Held twice each working day at 10:30 a.m. and 3:00 p.m. in the City of London.

Gold FRA   Gold Lease Forward Rate Agreement. Similar to a GOFRA but it is restricted solely to gold interest rates hedging with settlement in gold. A hedging product that is popular with those who have gold borrowing or deposit requirements. Goldfras are generally settled against the benchmark of U.S. dollar LIBOR minus the GOFO mean on the observation date.

Gold Loan   The provision of finance in gold for a gold-related project or business, typically in mining or jewelry inventory finance, which provides a combination of generally inexpensive funding together with built-in hedging.

Gold Parity   Legally fixed quantity of gold to which a monetary unit is pegged.

Gold Pool   The gold pool was an alliance between the central banks of Britain, Belgium, France, Italy, the Netherlands, Switzerland, the United States, and West Germany from 1961 to 1968 that endeavored to maintain the gold price at $35 per troy ounce.

Gold/Silver Ratio   The number of ounces of silver that can be bought with one ounce of gold.

Gold Standard   A monetary system with a fixed price for gold, and with gold coin either forming the whole circulation of currency within a country or with notes representing and redeemable in gold.

Gold Warrant

1. A warrant giving the buyer the right to buy gold at a specific price on a specified value date, for which the buyer pays a premium. While similar in structure to options, warrants are securitized instruments.

2. A certificate often issued by exchanges indicating ownership of physical metal.

Good Delivery   The specification that a gold or silver bar or a platinum or palladium ingot or plate must meet in order to be acceptable for delivery in a particular terminal market or futures exchange.

Grain   One of the earliest units of weight for gold, one grain being the equivalent of one grain of wheat taken from the middle of the ear: 1 grain = 0.0648 grams or 0.002083 troy ounces; 15.43 grains = 1 gram; 480.6 grains = 1 troy ounce; 24 grains = one pennyweight. (See also **Granules**.)

Granules   Bullion, including its various alloys presented for sale in granulated form, often referred to as grain.

Guinea   British gold coin with a nominal value of one pound first issued in 1663 and named after gold from Guinea in West Africa. It was unofficially revalued at 21 shillings at The Great Recoinage of 1696, a value confirmed in 1717. It has a fineness of 916.6 and a fine gold content of approximately one-quarter of a troy ounce.

Hallmark A mark or number of marks made on gold, silver, or platinum jewelry and other fabricated products to confirm that the quality is of the fineness marked on the item. See Web site: www.theg oldsmiths.co.uk

Head and Shoulders A three-peak pattern resembling the head and shoulders outline of a person, which is used to chart stock and commodity price trends. The pattern indicates the reversal of a trend. As prices move down to the right shoulder, a head and shoulders top is formed, meaning that prices should be falling. A reverse head and shoulders pattern has the head formation at the bottom of the chart and means that prices should be rising.

Hedge A transaction entered into in order to offset the impact of adverse price movements of an asset.

Historic Volatility Mathematically derived from price fluctuations of the underlying asset over a past specified period of time.

IBMA The International Bullion Master Agreement, issued by the LBMA in 1994.

IFEMA International Foreign Exchange Master Agreement.

IMF The International Monetary Fund was conceived at the Bretton Woods Conference in 1944 to promote international monetary cooperation and stability. It opened in Washington, D.C. in 1947. Web site: www.imf.org

Implied Volatility Volatility as calculated by determining the variable in the Black-Scholes option price formula from market option prices. The element of the formula that identifies the degree of supply and demand for options.

IMRO The Investment Management Regulatory Organisation (an SRO), superseded by the Financial Services Authority in 2001.

In the Money   Refers to options with intrinsic value. For example, calls where the strike price is less than the underlying asset price or puts where the strike price is greater than the underlying asset price.

Intrinsic Value   Refers to options. The difference between the current spot price and the option strike (or exercise) price, i.e., the in-the-money element.

Iridium   Chemical symbol Ir. Its specific gravity is 22.50 and its melting point is 1,539 degrees centigrade.

ISDA   The International Swaps & Derivatives Association. Web site: www.isda.org

ISDA Master Agreement   The International Swaps and Derivatives Association (ISDA) over-the-counter derivatives master agreement was drawn up by the New York–based trade association in 1987, revised in 1992, and again updated in 2002.

ISDA Bullion Definitions   An addendum to the ISDA Master Agreement developed in 1997 by ISDA and the LBMA to cover bullion terms. The 2005 ISDA Commodity Definitions incorporates the 1997 ISDA Bullion Definitions with some revisions.

Islands   In technical analysis, an island top is formed when a market gaps up and then gaps down during an uptrend to leave an isolated trading session. An island bottom is found at the base of a downtrend. Islands are regarded as a reversal pattern.

Istanbul Gold Exchange   The Istanbul Gold Exchange was founded in 1995. Web site: www.iab.gov.tr

Jakarta Futures Exchange (Pt. Bursa Berjangka Jakarta)   The JFX was established in August 1999. Web site: www.bbj-jfx.com

Japanese Candlestick Theory   The principles were developed in Japan during the 17th century by Munehisa Homma, a rice broker. Similarly to a bar chart, a candle chart uses the open, high, low, and closing prices, however, in a candle chart a body is created between the opening and closing prices. The bodies are presented in different colors to highlight the session's direction, usually a white body for an up day (open above the close) and a black body for a down session (close below the open). Regarded as good short-term signals.

Kam   Chinese for gold.

Key Reversal   In technical analysis, a crucial change in price direction, signaling an end to either a bull or bear market.

Kilo Bar   A popular small gold bar. A one-kilogram bar .995 fine = 31.990 troy ounces, and a one-kilogram bar 999.9 fine = 32.148 troy ounces.

Knock-In   In options, an exotic option in which the option becomes valid only when a predetermined price level (usually different to the strike price) is touched during the lifetime of the option.

Knock-Out   An exotic option that is automatically terminated or "knocked out" if the price of the underlying asset reaches a predetermined level (usually different to the strike price) during the lifetime of the option.

Koala   Australian platinum coin with a fineness of 999.5.

Krugerrand   South African gold coin first issued in 1967 with a fineness of 916.6.

Lakh (or lac)   Indian term for 100,000. Frequently used to describe silver or gold orders.

LBMA   The London Bullion Market Association was formally incorporated on December 14, 1987 to represent the interests of the participants in the wholesale bullion market and to encourage the development of the London market. Web site: www.lbma.org.uk

Leverage   See **Gearing**.

Limit Order   An order that has restrictions placed on it. The customer specifies a price and the order can only be executed if the market moves to or betters that price.

Glossary of Terms

Liquidity   The market tradability of an asset. A highly liquid market has a large number of buyers and sellers, or lenders, making it easy to enter or exit.

Loco   The place—location—at which a commodity, e.g., loco London gold, is physically held.

LBMA Good Delivery List   List of acceptable refiners of gold and silver whose bars meet the required standard (of fineness, weight, marks, and appearance) of the London Bullion Market Association.

Long   A long position means the purchase and retention of an asset.

Long Straddle   The purchase of call and put options with the same exercise price and expiry date. The investor expects a significant increase in volatility; direction of prices is not of prime importance.

Lookback Option   A history-dependent option where the settlement at maturity is reliant not only on whether the option is in-the-money at expiry, but also on the maximum or minimum price achieved by the underlying asset during at least some part of the option life.

LOT   Commonly used word for a standard futures contract.

LPPM   The London Platinum and Palladium Market was formalized by a Deed of Establishment in 1987 and represents the interests of the participants in the wholesale platinum and palladium markets and encourages the development of the London and Zurich markets. Web site: www.lppm.co.uk.

LPPM Good Delivery Lists   Lists of acceptable refiners of platinum and palladium whose plates and ingots meet the required standard (of fineness, weight, marks, and appearance) of the London Platinum and Palladium Market.

MACD (Moving Convergence/Divergence Momentum Indicator)
Usually the difference between the 26-day and 12-day exponential moving averages, although these parameters can be altered. A positive MACD indicates the 12-day average is above the 26-day average and

highlights a positive period and/or trend. The opposite holds true for a negative reading and a downtrend.

Maple Leaf   Canadian gold coin with a fineness of 999.9 or platinum coin with a fineness of 999.5.

Margin   Deposit, or collateral, required as security against open positions in futures, forwards, or options markets. Also called "Initial Margin" or "Original Margin."

Margin Call   The request for additional funds to cover losses on forward or futures contracts where the price has moved against a client. Also see **Variation Margin**.

Market Order   An order given to a dealer for immediate execution, to buy or sell at the best prevailing price. Also known as "At Best" or "At Market."

Mark to Market   The revaluation of a position at current market price levels.

MCX   Multi-Commodity Exchange of India Ltd. Headquartered in Mumbai, MCX is a demutualized multicommodity futures exchange. The exchange began operations in November 2003. Web site: www.mcxindia.com

Min/Max (Minimum/Maximum)   A zero cost collar-style hedging strategy whereby a client sells one option in exchange for another. In bullion markets, primarily used by producers who grant call options in exchange for put options; in this case, the structure guarantees that the client will receive a minimum predetermined price in exchange for a possible opportunity loss if the actual price at maturity is above a maximum level, as determined by the strike price of the call option granted.

Moving Average   In technical analysis, this is a key trend line that is plotted on a bar chart, reflecting the progress of prices over a given period of time. (See also **Weighted Moving Average**.)

Naked Option   The sale of an option by a party who does not hold the underlying asset to back it. See **Covered Option**.

Napoleon   French gold coin with a face value of 20 francs, bearing a portrait of Napoleon I or Napoleon III. It had a fineness of 900 and a fine gold content of 0.1867 troy ounces.

NCDEX   National Commodity and Derivatives Exchange. An online multicommodity exchange located in Mumbai, it began operations in December 2003. Web site: www.ncdex.com

Noble   Isle of Man platinum coin with a fineness of 999.5.

Numismatics   The specialized sector of the coin business for the study and collection of rare coins and other media of exchange, particularly those with archaeological and historic interest.

NYMEX   A U.S. futures exchange consisting of two divisions, NYMEX (the New York Mercantile Exchange) and COMEX (the Commodities Exchange). Web site: www.nymex.com

Offer   The price at which a dealer is willing to sell.

Open Interest   On a futures exchange, the daily statistic that indicates the number of open contracts, i.e., those that have not been fulfilled or closed out.

Open Outcry   A style of trading conducted on a futures exchange in a ring or a pit where dealers face each other, calling out the price, contract, month, and number of contracts.

Open Position   A market position that has not been closed out.

Option   An option is the right but not the obligation to buy and sell a predetermined quantity of an underlying asset at a predetermined price by or on a defined date.

Ore   Originally from the Old English for crude or unwrought metal. It refers to any economic mineral deposit of precious or other metals.

Osmium   Chemical symbol Os. Its specific gravity is 22.50 and its melting point is 2,700 degrees centigrade.

OTC   Over-the-Counter. Transactions that are quoted and conducted between parties on a principal-to-principal basis as opposed to being traded via a broker on an exchange.

OTC Option Over-the-Counter options are not traded on recognized future exchanges but between organizations acting as principals, or between a bank and its client.

Out of the Money Refers to options with only time value (i.e., no intrinsic value); e.g., calls where the strike price is greater than the underlying asset price or puts where the strike price is less than the underlying price.

Overbought A market in which the price, under excessive buying pressure, has risen too high and too fast without genuine fundamental support to maintain the new level.

Oversold A market that has fallen too far and too fast under excessive selling pressure and is expected to move back to a higher, more neutral level.

Palladium A metallic element, chemical symbol Pd. Its specific gravity is 12.00, and its melting point is 1,555 degrees centigrade.

Palladium Fixing Held twice each working day at 9:45 a.m. and 2:00 p.m. in the City of London.

Panda Chinese gold coin of 999.9 quality, first made in 1982.

Panning The classic and simple method of mining alluvial gold.

Paper Gold A term used to describe gold contracts such as loco London deals and futures contracts that do not necessarily involve the delivery of physical gold.

Pennyweight Originally the weight of a silver penny in Britain in the Middle Ages, which is still widely used in North America as the unit of weight in the jewelry trade: 20 pennyweights = 1 troy ounce.

Philharmoniker Austrian gold coin of 999.9 fineness, first issued in 1989.

PIA The Personal Investment Authority took over from LAUTRO and FIMBRA in 1994 as an **SRO** for most firms conducting investment business with the private investor. It was superseded by the **FSA** in 2001 when **FSMA** came into force.

Platinum   Chemical symbol Pt. Its specific gravity is 21.45 and melting point is 1,773 degrees centigrade.

Platinum Fixing   Held twice each working day at 9:45 a.m. and 2:00 p.m. in the City of London.

Platinum Group Metals   Platinum, palladium, iridium, osmium, rhodium, and ruthenium.

Precious Metals   Metals of great value being gold, silver, platinum, palladium, and other platinum group metals.

Put Option   A contract that gives the buyer the right, but not the obligation, to sell a specified amount of an asset at a predetermined price on or before a specified date.

Put Spread   An options position comprised of the purchase of a put option at one level and the sale of a put option at some lower level. The premium received by selling one option reduces the cost of buying the other, but participation is limited if the underlying goes down.

Quartation   The process in which silver is separated from gold by dissolving it out with nitric acid, more commonly referred to as nitric acid parting.

Refining   The separating and purifying of precious metals from other metals.

Resistance   In technical analysis, the price level where selling is expected to emerge.

Rho   A measure of an option's sensitivity to a change in interest rates; this will impact on both the future price of the option and the time value of the premium. Its impact increases with the maturity of the option.

Rhodium   Chemical symbol Rh. Its specific gravity is 12.44 and its melting point is 1,966 degrees centigrade.

Risk   The exposure to adverse market movements, mischance, or the possibility of losing money.

Rolled Gold   The process in which a layer of carat gold alloy is mechanically bonded to another metal.

RSI (Relative Strength Index)   Developed by J. Welles Wilder, the RSI compares the magnitude of an instrument's gains to its losses over a set period (usually 14 days). This is a momentum oscillator and provides information such as overbought or oversold conditions and divergence between price and indicator.

Ruthenium   Chemical symbol Ru. Its specific gravity is 12.20 and its melting point is 2,500 degrees centigrade.

Scrap Gold   The broad term for any gold that is sent back to a refiner or processor for recycling.

Sell Signal   In technical analysis, a chart pattern that indicates a key reversal downwards in price.

Settlement Date   The date on which a contract must be fully paid for and delivered. It is the general practice in international precious metals markets for settlement to take place two business days after the transaction date, i.e., spot.

Settlement Price   In futures markets, the price that is set by the exchange committee at the end of each trading day and that is used by the clearinghouse to market open positions and assess margin calls.

Settlement Risk   The risk that arises when payments are not exchanged simultaneously, generally arising because of time differences. One party to a transaction must effect payment or delivery in an earlier time zone without having confirmation of the receipt of a reciprocal asset in a later time zone.

SFA   The Securities and Futures Authority (an **SRO**) was responsible for the regulation of investment business in the United Kingdom. It was superseded by the FSA in 2001 when the FSMA came into force.

Shanghai Gold Exchange   The Shanghai Gold Exchange was founded in 2002. Web site: www.sge.sh

Shanghai Futures Exchange   The Shanghai Futures Exchange was formed in December 1999. Web site: www.shfe.com

Short   A short position means the sale of an asset not yet owned.

Short Straddle   The sale of a call and put option with the same exercise price and expiry date. The investor has a neutral view of the underlying asset and expects limited price fluctuation.

Silver   Latin name *Argentum*. The chemical symbol is Ag, specific gravity is 10.49, and the melting point is 960 degrees centigrade.

Silver Fixing   Held each working day at 12:00 p.m. in the City of London.

Singapore Exchange Limited (SGX)   The Singapore Exchange was inaugurated on December 1, 1999, following the merger of the Stock Exchange of Singapore (SES) and the Singapore International Monetary Exchange (SIMEX). Web site: www.sgx.com

Smelting   The process of melting ores or concentrates to separate out the metal content from impurities.

Souk   The local name for *market* used throughout the Arab world.

Sovereign   British gold coin with face value of one pound sterling, a fineness of 916.6, and a fine gold content of 0.2354 troy ounces.

Spot Settlement   Delivery of metal and payment of money, which takes place two business days after the transaction date.

Spot Deferred   Hybrid forward contract offering floating interest rates and no fixed delivery. It is more flexible than conventional spot or forward contracts.

SROs   Self Regulatory Organizations were established under the Financial Services Act of 1986 to carry out the regulation of most institutions involved in investment activities in the United Kingdom. Under **FSMA**, the role played by the SROs was taken over by the **FSA** in 2001.

Standard Bar/Plate/Ingot   Refers to any of the following:

1. Gold bar weighing approximately 400 ounces or 12.5 kilograms and having a minimum fineness of 995 parts per 1,000 pure gold.

2. Silver bar weighing approximately 1,000 ounces with a minimum fineness of 999.

3. Platinum or palladium plate or ingot between 1 and 6 kilograms with a minimum fineness of 999.5.

Standard Deviation   Statistical measure of the degree to which an individual value in a probability distribution tends to vary from the mean of the distribution. Indicates probability of a variable or price falling within a certain width or band around the mean.

Stochastics   Developed by George Lane, this momentum oscillator shows the location of the current close relative to the high/low range over a specified period. Closing levels near the top of the range indicate buying pressure, while closing levels near the base of the range indicate selling pressure.

Stop Loss   An order placed to liquidate an open position when the price reaches a specified level in order to prevent further losses. These orders are only handled on a "best efforts" basis, as there is no guarantee that an order can be executed at the specified price if the market is highly volatile and prices move so fast, or "gap," that the order cannot be carried out at the price requested.

Straddle   Purchase or sale of call and put options for the same underlying asset with the same expiry date and strike price.

Strangle   In options, a speculative strategy of either buying or selling puts and calls, each with the same expiry date but with different strike prices.

Strike Price   In options, the predetermined price at which an option may be exercised.

Glossary of Terms

Support In technical analysis, the price level where new buyers are expected to emerge.

Swap Refers to any of the following:

1. Simultaneous purchase and sale of spot against forward.

2. An exchange between different locations.

3. A swap or exchange of different size of quality of bullion bars or platinum and/or palladium ingots or plates.

4. An agreement whereby a floating price is exchanged for a fixed price over a specified period.

Switch Simultaneous purchase and sale of the same asset for different maturity dates.

Tael Traditional Chinese unit of weight for gold: one tael = 1.20337 troy ounces = 37.4290 grams. The nominal fineness of a Hong Kong tael bar is 990 but in Taiwan 5- and 10-tael bars can be 999.9 fine.

Technical Analysis The study of historical prices, examining patterns of price change, rates of change, and changes in volume of trading and open interest, in order to predict future price behavior. Technical analysis is usually performed in chart or graph form.

Theta In options, the rate of change in the value of the option with respect to time with all else remaining the same.

Time Value Refers to options. The difference between an option's market price and its intrinsic value.

Tola Traditional Indian unit of weight for gold: One tola = 0.375 troy ounces = 11.6638 grams. The most popular sized bar is 10 tola = 3.75 troy ounces. Weights are for 999.9 gold purity.

Tokyo Commodities Exchange TOCOM was established on November 1,1984 as a merger of the Tokyo Textile Exchange, the Tokyo Rubber Exchange, and the Tokyo Gold Exchange. Web site: www.tocom.or.jp

Tom/Next   Refers to the time period commencing one business day forward from the present and ending one business day later (usually spot). In precious metals, generally refers to the swap rate for borrowing or lending metal versus U.S. dollars for this time period, which is typically used to manage short-term liquidity flows.

Trend/Trend Line   In technical analysis, trend is defined as a directional move over a period of time. There are three types: up, down, and sideways. A trend line is a straight line that connects two or more price points, extending it into the future to act as a support or resistance. Trend lines are important in that they identify and confirm trends. (See also **Support** and **Resistance.**)

Troy Ounce   The traditional unit of weight used for precious metals, which was attributed to a weight used in Troyes, France, in medieval times: one troy ounce is equal to 1.0971428 ounces avoirdupois.

Unallocated Account   An account where specific bars are not set aside and the customer has a general entitlement to the metal. This is the most convenient, cheapest, and most commonly used method of holding metal. The holder is an unsecured creditor.

Underlying   The variable on which a futures, option, or other derivative contract is based.

Value Date   The date agreed between parties for the settlement of a transaction.

Vanilla Option   A standard transaction that is not tailored to the needs of either party. A plain vanilla option pays out the difference between the strike price of the option and the spot price of the underlying at the time of the exercise.

Variation Margin   Additional margin, or collateral payable by an investor, resulting from an adverse movement in the price of the underlying asset in a forward, futures, or options contract.

Vega   A measure of how much an option's price will change as the volatility of the underlying fluctuates.

Volatility   Refers to options. The rate of change in the price of the underlying asset. (See also **Implied Volatility** and **Historic Volatility.**)

Volume   On futures exchanges, the number of contracts traded in a session.

Vreneli   Swiss gold coin with a face value of 20 francs issued as legal tender in the period from 1897 to 1935. It had a fineness of 900 and a fine gold content of 0.1867 troy ounces.

Wafer   Small, thin gold bars popular in the Middle East, South East Asia, and Japan.

Warehouse Receipt   A warehouse or depository receipt is issued when delivery is taken on a futures exchange. It specifies the quantity and fineness of the precious metal held.

Weighted Moving Average   Used in technical analysis, a weighted moving average gives a greater weighting to more recent price data, as opposed to a simple moving average that gives equal weighting to all prices. (See also **Moving Average.**)

White Gold   A gold alloy containing whitening agents such as silver, palladium, or nickel as well as other base metals, often used as a setting for diamond jewelry.

Writer   In options, the seller or granter of the option.

Yield Curve   The relationship between interest rate yields and maturity lengths. The yield curve normally has a positive slope (i.e., upwards) because yields on long-term interest rates usually exceed short-term yields. An investor expects a higher return for holding an asset for a longer time, hence yields normally increase with maturity length.

Zero-Cost Option   An option strategy under which one option is purchased by simultaneously selling another option of equal value. (See also **Min/Max.**)

Properties of Gold

Courtesy of World Gold Council

(www.gold.org)

 Gold, (symbol Au) has an atomic number of 79, i.e., each gold atom has 79 protons in its nucleus. The atomic mass of the gold atom is 196.967 and the atomic radius is 0.1442 nanometers. Interestingly this is smaller than would be predicted by theory.

The arrangement of outer electrons around the gold nucleus is related to gold's characteristic yellow color. The color of a metal is based on transitions of electrons between energy bands. The conditions for the intense absorption of light at the wavelengths necessary to produce the typical gold color are fulfilled by a transition from the d band to unoccupied positions in the conduction band. Gold's attractive warm color has led to its widespread use in decoration

While the number of protons in a gold nucleus is fixed at 79, the number of neutrons can vary from one atom to another giving a number of isotopes of gold. However, there is only one stable nonradioactive isotope accounting for all naturally found gold.

The crystal structure for metallic gold is face-centered cubic (FCC). See Figure IV–1.

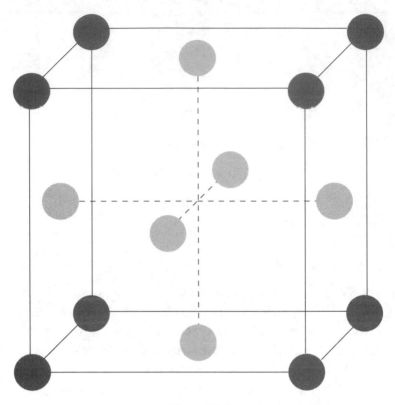

Figure IV–1
The Crystal Structure of Metallic Gold

This crystal structure contributes to gold's very high ductility since FCC lattices are particularly suitable for allowing the movement of dislocations in the lattice. Such dislocation movement is essential for achieving high ductility.

The density of gold (19.3 grams per cubic centimeter) depends on both its atomic mass and the crystal structure. This makes gold rather heavy compared to some other common materials. For example, aluminum has a density of 2.7 grams per cubic centimeter, and even steel's density is only 7.87 grams per cubic centimeter.

The melting point of pure gold is 1,064 degrees centigrade, although when alloyed with other elements such as silver or copper the gold alloy will melt over a range of temperatures. The boiling point of gold, when gold transforms from the liquid to gaseous state, is 2,860 degrees centigrade.

The ability of gold to efficiently transfer heat and electricity is bettered only by copper and silver, but unlike these metals gold does not tarnish, making it indispensable in electronics.

The electrical resistivity of gold is 0.022 micro-ohm per meter at 20 degrees centigrade. The thermal conductivity is 310 watts per meter per kelvin at the same temperature. The corrosion resistance of gold is perhaps one of its most useful properties. Electrode potentials are a useful method for representing the tendency of a metal to corrode. Electrode potentials are measured with reference to hydrogen, and an electrochemical series can be prepared for metals as indicated in Table IV–1. Not surprisingly, gold is at the top of the series indicating its high corrosion resistance. In practice, it is corroded only by a mixture of nitric and hydrochloric acid (aqua regia). In everyday use gold does not tarnish.

Table IV–1
Electrode Potentials for Various Metals

ELECTRODE POTENTIAL (VOLTS)	ELEMENT
+1.5	Gold
+0.8	Silver
−0.4	Iron
−0.8	Zinc
−1.66	Aluminum

The metal gold is extremely malleable (the extent to which a material can undergo deformation in compression before failure). In the annealed state it can be hammered cold into a translucent wafer

0.000013 centimeters thick. One ounce of gold can be beaten into a sheet covering over 9 square meters and 0.000018 centimeters thick.

Gold is also ductile (degree of extension that takes place before failure of a material in tension) and one ounce can be drawn into 80 km (50 miles) of thin gold wire (5 microns diameter) to make electrical contacts and bonding wire.

The Young's modulus of elasticity of a material is related to rigidity or stiffness and is defined as the ratio between the stress applied and the elastic strain it produces. Gold has a Young's modulus of 79 giga pascals, which is very similar to silver, but significantly lower than iron or steel.

Hardness is defined as the ability of a material to resist surface abrasion. The relative hardness of materials was historically assessed using a list of materials arranged in such order that any material in the list will scratch any one below it. Thus, diamond, the hardest substance known, heads the list with a hardness index of 10 while talc is at the bottom with a hardness index of 1. On this scale, gold has a value of 2.5 to 3, i.e., it is a soft metal. For more accurate measurements the Vickers hardness measurement (Hv) is used and gold has a value of approximately 25 Hv in the annealed condition.

Gold demonstrates excellent biocompatibility within the human body (the main reason for its use as a dental alloy), and as a result there are a number of direct applications of gold as a medical material. Gold also possesses a high degree of resistance to bacterial colonization and because of this it is the material of choice for implants that are at risk of infection, such as those in the inner ear.

Gold forms a number of interesting compounds based on the familiar oxidation states $+1$ and $+3$. Gold-based chemicals include halides, cyanides, and sulfides.

The basic properties of gold are listed in Table IV–2 on the next page.

Properties of Gold

Table IV–2
Properties of Gold

PROPERTY	CHARACTERISTIC
Atomic weight	196.97
Atomic number	79
Number of naturally occurring isotopes	1
Melting point (degrees centigrade)	1064
Crystal structure	FCC
Density (grams per cubic centimeter)	19.3
Thermal conductivity (watts per meter per kelvin)	310
Electrical resistivity (micro-ohm per meter at 20 degrees centigrade)	0.022
Young's modulus (giga pascals)	79
Hardness (Hv)	25
Tensile stress (mega pascal)	124
0.2 % proof stress (mega pascal)	30
Poissons ratio	0.42

APPENDIX

V

Bar Weights and Their Agreed Fine Gold Content

GROSS WEIGHT	FINE GOLD CONTENT IN OUNCES TROY PER BAR		
	995.0 ASSAY	**999.0 ASSAY**	**999.9 ASSAY**
1 kilogram	31.990	32.119	32.148
0.5 kilogram	15.995	16.059	16.074
0.25 kilogram	7.998	8.030	8.037
200 grams	6.398	6.424	6.430
100 grams	3.199	3.212	3.215
50 grams	1.600	1.607	1.608
20 grams	0.640	0.643	0.643
10 grams	0.321	0.322	0.322
5 grams	0.161	0.161	0.161
100 ounces	99.500	99.900	99.990
50 ounces	49.750	49.950	49.995
25 ounces	24.875	24.975	24.998
10 ounces	9.950	9.990	9.999
5 ounces	4.975	4.995	5.000
1 ounces	0.995	0.999	1.000
10 tolas	3.731	3.746	3.750
5 taels	5.987	6.011	6.017

Index

Index

Index

Index

Index

Index

Index

Index

Index

Index

Index

About the Author

Jonathan Spall is director of commodities at Barclays Capital, the investment banking arm of Barclays Bank. He has over 25 years experience in gold and related markets, including working nine years in Asia/Pacific.